D1609831

FIRST LIGHT

FIRST LIGHT

The Explosive Memoirs
of a British Army ATO

Paul Wharton

Book Guild Publishing
Sussex, England

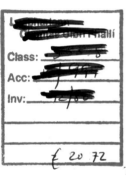

Class:
Acc:
Inv:

£ 20 72

Published in Great Britain in 2012 by
The Book Guild Ltd
Pavilion View
19 New Road
Brighton, BN1 1UF

First published in 2009 by Brisance Books
Copyright © Paul Wharton 2009, 2012

The right of Paul Wharton to be identified as the author of this
work has been asserted by him in accordance with the
Copyright, Designs and Patents Act 1988.

All rights reserved. No part of this publication may be reproduced,
transmitted, or stored in a retrieval system, in any form or by any
means, without permission in writing from the publisher, nor be
otherwise circulated in any form of binding or cover other than that
in which it is published and without a similar condition being
imposed on the subsequent purchaser.

Printed and bound in Great Britain by
CPI Group (UK) Ltd, Croydon, CR0 4YY

A catalogue record for this book is available from
The British Library

ISBN 978 1 84624 653 1

Contents

CONTENTS

Dedication

This book is dedicated to the memory and also the families of those members of 321 EOD Company, RAOC, who were killed as a result of enemy action.

Operators

Capt. Stewardson	(29)	9th Sept 1971
WO2 Davies	(38)	4th Nov 1971
SSgt Cracknell	(29)	15th March 1972
Sgt Butcher	(24)	15th March 1972
Major Calladene	(39)	29th March 1972
Capt. Young	(27)	15th July 1972
WO2 Clark	(34)	3rd Aug 1972
SSgt Hills	(28)	5th Dec 1972
Capt. Gritten	(29)	21st June 1973
SSgt Beckett	(36)	30th Aug 1973
SSgt Brammah	(31)	18th Feb 1974
SSgt Rose	(30)	7th Nov 1974
WO2 Maddocks	(32)	2nd Dec 1974
WO2 Garside	(34)	17th July 1975
Sgt Walsh	(28)	9th Jan 1977
WO2 O'Neill	(34)	31st May 1981
WO2 Howard	(29)	8th July 1988

In Support

Cpl Brown	(25)	17th July 1975
Sig Reece	(18)	2nd Aug 1979
Gnr Furminger	(19)	2nd Aug 1979

Abbreviations

ATO	Ammunition Technical Officer
CATO	Chief Ammunition Technical Officer
CO	Commanding Officer
COP	Close Observation Platoon
CSE	Combined Services Entertainment
ECM	Electronic Counter Measures
EOD	Explosive Ordnance Disposal
GOC	General Officer Commanding
HME	Home-Made Explosive
IED	Improvised Explosive Device
IEDD	Improvised Explosive Device Disposal
MID	Mentioned in Despatches
MoD	Ministry of Defence
NB	Nitrobenzene
NTH	Newtownhamilton
PIRA	Provisional Irish Republican Army
RAOC	Royal Army Ordnance Corps
RC	Radio controlled
RCV	Remote Control Vehicle
RE	Royal Engineer
RESA	Royal Engineer Search Adviser
REST	Royal Engineer Search Team
RGJ	Royal Green Jackets
RNAD	Royal Navy Armaments Depot
RPG	Rocket Propelled Grenade
RSP	Render Safe Procedure
RUC	Royal Ulster Constabulary
RV	Rendezvous
SAS	Special Air Service/Special Ammunition Stowage
SATO	Senior Ammunition Technical Officer
SF	Security Forces
TPU	Time and Power Unit
UDR	Ulster Defence Regiment
WIS	Weapons Intelligence Section, Royal Military Police
XMG	Crossmaglen
MBTI	Myers-Briggs (*personality*) Type Indicator

For my parents who guided me
For Jen who had to wait for me
For my children who fulfil me
For Ros who enriches me

PREFACE

One autumnal evening, as I idly sifted through my bomb disposal reports, memorabilia and disintegrating photo album, the build-up to the 5th November annual battlefest was gathering pace outside the house. It doesn't happen too often, and a whiff of gunpowder is quite different to the pungent stench of blasted high explosives, yet this time it was enough to bring my previous life back into focus. That evening, amid the intermittent flash and thud of fireworks, I sat and thought again of those cold boggy fields of South Armagh, which had dragged at our vehicles as they skidded and strained to haul out, or just to move, the highly hazardous loads I had tethered to the end of a long rope; where each gateway and every gap in the myriad of grey stone walls was potentially lethal; where tinkling brooks disappeared into deadly culverts; who of us with this experience could forget the adrenalin-high excitement of the current job? Without too much effort my nose might again wrinkle at the overpowering carcinogenic reek of a home-made explosive (HME) that smelled of marzipan and impregnated everything it touched. I imagined I could hear the ribald joking and laughter of the people I lived and worked with and conversely it would be so easy, even now, to weep for good people devastated by the conflict's cruel ironies.

The thirty-year Irish conflict was much more intense than many people on the mainland probably realise. A total of 3,350 British people were killed and a further 47,500 injured. In just one year, 1972, at the very apex of the violence, terrorists succeeded in killing 100 British soldiers and wounding 500 more. In 1972 six of those deaths were Bomb Disposal Operators.

Today I work for a major pharmaceutical wholesaler in a job where risk is also a key factor, but any failure is a cost borne by the bottom line. It doesn't have the same serious and devastating repercussions on my family. Yes, it's a different world from the one my colleagues and I inhabited all those years ago.

In deciding to publish my army experiences, my initial intention had been to provide my family with a narrative of what it was like to have been a Bomb Disposal Operator during the Northern Ireland campaign. Thrown into a box with the rest of my military memorabilia, the book might surface one day to put all the accompanying bits and bobs into some sort of context. Whilst my first attempt at a book might just have achieved that aim, this second edition fleshes out my journey to become an Ammunition Technician and goes on to provide a more rounded picture of the type of work for which the profession is responsible. I hope my own experiences will paint a context for the work, what it entailed and the unstable, volatile nature of it all.

As with the first book, this edition also provides an opportunity to highlight something that vexed me for a very long time. Why is it that none of the seventeen Royal Army Ordnance Corps Bomb Disposal Operators killed during the Northern Ireland Campaign were awarded a posthumous gallantry medal? Not one of them was *recognised* in this way. It appears to be a question that dare not speak its name. This anomaly stands out even more starkly when compared to others killed in similar circumstances over a similar period. In London, a George Cross and George Medal were awarded to two members of the Metropolitan Police Bomb Squad killed attempting to neutralise IRA devices. Similarly, in the Falklands Campaign, a Navy Conspicuous Gallantry Medal was awarded to the Royal Engineer Bomb Disposal Operator who lost his life attempting to defuse an Argentinean aircraft bomb onboard a ship. In fact, almost every large war-time bomb defused by the Royal Engineers results in a formal recognition for their operators. Yet, if you were to ask most people to hazard a guess as to what is more dangerous to the man defusing it – a 500kg iron bomb with a military fuse or a 5kg explosive device with an improvised firing mechanism – I doubt that the iron bomb would come out on top as often as the improvised bomb. I'm not saying that all unexploded iron bombs are safe, I'm simply pointing out what I see as an anomaly in how 'the system' recognised our efforts. One can't help but notice that citations are more easily written and approval obtained once the media is on the case – as it is today in Afghanistan where the work has now achieved a very high profile. It begs the following question, doesn't it? Can it really be that the number of TV cameras and journalists at a bomb incident is a measure of an operator's gallantry? Discuss!

For me, the big question arising from the Ulster campaign is, well, just how did this matter get missed? Was the bar set too high? Where was the media when it was needed? What makes this matter more difficult to accept today, considering the focus on the work in Afghanistan, is that no one at the time seemed to think they were acts worthy of recognition.

In order to recognise gallantry, which is displayed on our behalf, and be able to honour it appropriately, the system that underpins it should be effective. During the early Ulster campaign the medals system was, in fact, flawed, as I will explain later.

I would, therefore, want this book to say something about the men who died. It is not just about who they were, how, or even why most of them died; it's about the type of dangers they faced, which proved fatal for them and a catastrophe for their families. These hazards were faced by all members of my profession who served in this capacity and the book might also provide a testimony to many others whose contribution wasn't felt to be sufficiently worthy to be formally recognised by the system, but who also faced and dealt with the same dangers. You might conclude, just as I do, that it was just so easy to die if your luck abandoned you.

Some may think that the more time a person spends at this anti-terrorist work and the more experienced he is, the better at it he becomes; that any near-misses he experiences might add value to that experience and that applying these rules provides him with the best chance of making it through. But I would maintain that none of that is relevant if your luck eventually runs out on you. Everything you have learnt or experienced before will not protect you if at that crucial time, just once, you underestimate, interpret incorrectly or misunderstand what is in front of you. The more time you spend at this job, the greater the probability that this will happen. I had my share of misinterpretations and came close to disaster on more than one occasion, so I can say, with hand on heart, that I am here but for the grace of God...

Bomb Disposal Operators in the Northern Ireland conflict only had to serve two tours of duty as an Operator. It was enough.

ANOTHER BRICK IN THE WALL?

You don't know where life is going to take you. No one does. And no one who knew me as a child could ever have envisaged that I would have had the career I did. But getting on in life is not just about your childhood, education or money; it's more about ambition. If you have ambition and a reasonable amount of common sense, and you can apply it – after that it's down to chance. When you look back from the future you will see that any number of accidents got you to where you are – good and bad – and chance has definitely played a big part in my life – good and bad, but mostly good. I have no complaints.

Mum and Dad were married in 1950. They had met while Dad was serving at Wellington Barracks as a Lance Corporal in the Grenadier Guards. He'd joined up as he came of age during the war.

Taken in Syria 1946 with friends in the Grenadier Guards. My father is second in from the left. This is a brilliant photo, I love it.

Mum & Dad circa 1957. Insecure times in those early days.

I was born in 1951 and christened at the Guards' Chapel. A short time later, Dad left the army, feeling he'd done his 'stint', and we moved north to Blackpool to stay with Dad's family. By 1957, there were four of us and we lived in a single room at Auntie Nora and Uncle Alec's house. It wasn't ideal, but at least we weren't homeless. Mum was still homesick, missing her large family back in Wood Green where she had been born and raised. Undoubtedly there were pressures, but the trials and tribulations, which I expect accompanied this insecure existence, were fortunately pretty much invisible to me or my sister, Gill.

It was around this time that I experienced my first exposure to explosives, and it was a somewhat traumatic experience for everyone involved. Of course it was bonfire night and a crackling, roaring bonfire dominated the small garden at 85 Patterdale Avenue. I was with my mother in the kitchen as the adults set off fireworks closer to the house than was probably advisable. Suddenly, with a whoosh and a bang, a rocket ricocheted off the part-open window, struck the kitchen ceiling and, still whooshing, landed in a box of fireworks minding its own business on the kitchen table. Immediately, the kitchen was Dante's inferno. The pandemonium was great with the adults shouting advice and running around outside like headless chickens. There wasn't much they could do and my mother and I were too far from the safety of a doorway. Grabbing me, she pulled me down alongside a kitchen unit and just about smothered me in her protective embrace. Even so, I could just make out the flaming curtains and the top of the table as the tubes of magnesium and gunpowder banged and spat away like large demented rip raps. The roman candles were the most impressive, spitting off in every direction and bouncing back off the ceiling and walls.

Miraculously, no one was injured and the house didn't burn down. It was surely the most exciting bonfire night I'd ever attended. That one was only surpassed years later when my family and I attended the Towcester parish church firework display. This time the fireworks had been ever so diligently stored underneath a trestle table, which was unfortunately the platform for setting off fireworks. Needless to say, the fireworks under the table cooked off. The good people of Towcester scattered in all directions, grabbing their children as they ran, and no one was injured. But it was a close run thing, and having the local Bobby run the event had not reduced the risks. I avoid small firework displays today since, in the hands of enthusiastic amateurs, the events are potentially hazardous since the inherent dangers of powder explosives are commonly underestimated.

It took a leap of faith for my parents to decide to buy a house and a greater one for them to think that they could scrape together the money for a deposit. As good luck would have it, Dad's brother, Tom, joined the Merchant Navy and gave Dad his motorbike to sell. With the money, they bought a house in Poulton-le-Fylde, Lancashire: a three bedroom semi on one of many new estates that sprang up around the village at that time.

The street was pretty much a building site at the time, but we moved in on a sunny day in May 1958. My mother loved it and has lived there ever since.

Dad tried different jobs: process worker at Salwick near Preston, Co-op milkman, and he even had his own window cleaning and chimney sweeping businesses, but exacerbated by the mortgage, the financial hardships continued. On one occasion we even had bailiffs visit and catalogue our possessions when the repayments fell into arrears. Mum had to go out to work when, in those days, most women were pretty much chained to the house. I didn't like that too much; as a child I preferred her to be chained to the house, but needs must. Paradoxically, throughout this time, I don't recollect us actually being short of anything and Christmas was always a magical time. We made do, as people say. I guess our needs then were pretty unsophisticated. The money issue was eventually resolved when our neighbour, Ken Brown, recommended Dad for a job at the local ICI factory, and Dad worked shifts there until shortly before his death in 1981. He worked hard too, never taking a holiday that I can remember.

The one thing that I will always remember about Dad was that he liked to be first. We had the first telephone in our part of the street (which was a mistake because all the neighbours would drop in to use it), the first colour television and also the first central heating system installed. In those days these very useful things were considered the forefront of technology.

At this time, Poulton is a small bustling village. At its centre are the wooden stocks and an attractive parish church that stands atop the highest point around about: a gently contouring hill which is only really appreciated now via a relief map. The church graveyard is overgrown with a neglected look about it. Hundreds of years of weatherworn headstones are spread around like large spilled dominos. Poulton still has the odd cobbled street and many large empty buildings stand gloomily abandoned where time has left them far behind. At the bottom of Chapel Street is the red-bricked Wesleyan Methodist church, behind which is a large grain warehouse that always seems empty. On Tithebarn Street the original tithe buildings remain but, once again, have been allowed to decay. Opposite them is an imposing Georgian building which has also seen better days. Alongside that is the Hobby Crafts shop, which will, uniquely, still be doing business thirty years later. Looking across the road, the pavements are blighted by a garage that spews out black oil and grease. Alongside is an alleyway, down which a small confectionary factory emits a sweet smell that draws children to it. Small farms still exist close to the village, none of which look particularly prosperous. Cottage terraces and local wooded walks add to the country feel. Behind the Golden Ball public house young boys cluster on the tall smoke-stained wall at the back of the busy Monday morning cattle market. They eagerly await the numerous wheezing steam trains on what is a busy direct line between Blackpool and Euston. Clutching books of train numbers, they tick them off as the trains pass by. It's a popular hobby. In 1958 the village still has a market feel with green fields all around that separate it from its nearest big neighbour, Blackpool, a good three miles away.

Sadly, almost everything I've mentioned about the village, apart from the stocks, is doomed; the old buildings, the centre and adjoining roads will all undergo an extensive face lift in the sixties. At the end of which, Poulton's history will have been pretty much eradicated to meet the perceived needs of its burgeoning populace. Today, it has a shopping centre, car parks, over-stretched pubs, the mandatory one way system and countryside which is receding at an alarming pace.

Growing up in this benign environment enables me to stretch my youthful wings in all sorts of directions and the myriad woods and fields are adventure grounds for any child with an ounce of imagination. And so begins my experimentation with explosives. At the age of fourteen, experimenting with gunpowder is great fun. At first we only have access to this in the weeks leading up to bonfire night when fireworks are easily obtainable, but the breakthrough

Above: First Prize at Garstang Fair circa 1963. It's me on the cardboard saxophone with two class mates Stephen Gardner and Graham Meek. The Dave Clark 5 had recently knocked the Beatles off the number 1 spot so we were highly contemporary.

Left: This shattered pipe remained embedded in the railway fence at Cottam Hall Playing Fields for years afterwards. We treated them like fireworks but they were much more dangerous than that!

comes when a school friend, a bit of a boffin, John Collinson, obtains a recipe for an explosive, which utilises a common weed killer. With a saddle bag full of metal pipes packed with the mix, we traverse the countryside and Poulton rattles to sound barrier-type booms, as fences and trees bear the brunt of our destructive, albeit innocent, nature. We probably escaped death or injury by an inch; much later I would learn just how sensitive and, consequently, how dangerous such a compound can be.

Most mornings I would leave the house for school with a sick feeling in the pit of my stomach. I remember that feeling well. The text and exercise books I had jammed in my leather satchel the day before remained undisturbed. Too easily distracted and without any academic confidence, I couldn't motivate myself to put the effort it. And, let's face it, leaving school always seemed a million miles away. I remained in the A stream, but it's a mystery as to how.

Eight years of schooling run its course and, in 1966, adulthood beckons me. Walking away from Hodgson Secondary Modern School for the last time is a bit scary, unsettling. I had underachieved and now is the reckoning.

I had already tried to get into the RAF and spent a day at their recruitment centre at Stafford, but had been rejected due to my poor academic skills. Afterwards, a school teacher pointed me out to the class as a prime example of what happens if you don't work hard enough. He was probably right, but it was an embarrassing experience.

Everyone else in my form stays on to take O-levels, but I leave with hardly a fond farewell. I don't remember anyone of any importance suggesting that I

1966: My half hearted attempt to join the RAF. An Air Vice Marshall on a visit to the RAF Stafford Recruiting Centre stopped to chat and the RAF kindly sent me the **photo as a momento.**

should stay. I'm a fifteen-year-old *brick in the wall*.

The youth employment agency suggests I take up a job offer as a junior clerk at the ICI chemical and plastics works at Thornton Cleveleys. The ICI at this time is a giant of British Industry and a major employer in the area. Its Meccano-like infrastructure and towers of hissing steam dominate the River Wyre tributary for miles between Thornton and Fleetwood. They tell me that working as a clerk there could be a first step towards obtaining an apprenticeship with them and this seems like a good idea, since I don't have any other ideas.

Ken, my predecessor, having obtained an apprenticeship (hence the vacancy), is away to Welwyn Garden City for a couple of years to become an electrician. I inherit his job title, Clerk Messenger, Plastics Distribution, and it isn't long before I am in command of a desk, a black Imperial typewriter and a works bicycle.

There are no women at the office. Instead, it is filled with a medley of male clerks who beaver away all day chatting about women, football, TV and arranging deliveries and receipts and, I guess, a multitude of other things. Everyone is friendly and I quite enjoy it.

Four times a day I cycle the factory estate to collect hard copy delivery notes from the various departments and bring them back to the office. Just occasionally I bump into my dad as he works with the chemical tankers on the other side of the factory. This work can be hazardous and occasionally he gets a gassing, but I suppose he prefers this to the frost-bitten hands he received as a milkman.

Cycling around the factory I get to recognise two factory smells in particular: pear drops, which I'm told is phosgene gas, and 'swimming pool', which is of course chlorine. Every now and then a gas cloud magically appears, disguised as steam, and I have the misfortune to cycle into it. It might look like steam but the stuff grabs at my throat and I emerge choking and coughing with eyes streaming. I wonder how much of a person's lifespan could be debited by exposure to such things.

In between my bicycle rounds I type out labels for the samples of plastic the company distributes. Overall, it's not a bad job for which I'm paid the princely sum of £5 a week.

The late summer and autumn are pretty much a carefree period and there's plenty of thinking time out there on my bike. It dawns on me that if I'm not careful I could end my days here as a shift worker. I don't have anything against shift workers; I just need my sleep. Clues to indicate that I might not be in the right place are that I don't especially enjoy the night school or even the day release at Blackpool Technical College. It feels like school again. Frankly, I haven't got a hope of qualifying as an electrician, even if selected for an ICI apprenticeship. Not only that, on more than one occasion I get caught out skiving off and, for my tardiness, I'm rightly 'front and centred' by Mr Bradshaw and/or Mr France, and read the riot act. Before long I begin to hatch an escape plot.

At thirteen, I had joined the Air Training Corps whilst it had been a detached Flight based at the nearby village of Thornton Cleveleys. This set-up moved to Breck Road in Poulton and then, through a recruitment drive, which I helped to accomplish, it became an independent ATC Squadron in its own right. Not having been accepted by the RAF, therefore, had been a blow at the time, but with hindsight a lucky escape since I might just have enrolled for anything they had to offer.

The RAF wrote me a very nice letter afterwards inviting me to re-apply, but I decide to look elsewhere. I think about the adventures my dad recounted of his time in the army (it looked like he'd had a lot of fun) and, without telling anyone, I approach the nearest thing that the Fylde has to the Foreign Legion: the army careers office. The seeds of ambition, henceforth, are sown.

A letter soon arrives inviting me to Fulwood Barracks at Preston. Fulwood Barracks is the Headquarters of the Lancashire Infantry Regiment, the Loyals, and is also the regional recruitment centre.

Entering the barracks I'm surprised to bump into a guy called Stuart McGough, who I recognise from Hodgson School. He's dressed in olive drab fatigues, a black beret and, armed with a broom, he's sweeping the road. I hadn't even known he'd joined the army. We have a quick chat and then part company. I vow that I won't end up sweeping roads.

To measure my aptitude I take a load of written tests around logic spotting and reproducing patterns and (since this is not maths, science or geography) I fly through them. I get good results and the recruiting officer appears quite impressed. There and then I'm offered a choice of trades, but he's especially enthusiastic about a role called an Ammunition Technician. He tells me that it involves inspecting and repairing ammunition and disposing of explosives. It sounds exciting. He goes on to tell me that the minimum rank is corporal and so the pay is going to be good. It's very tempting, but I have in my head a job type that is portable to civilian life. I humour him and agree that Ammo Tech can be my third choice. I expect to get one of my other two selections, which are Fitter (internal combustion and pump) and Fitter (Plant).

The day the acceptance letter drops through the door is one of the happiest of my life. The fact that I've been offered my third choice cannot spoil my sense of achievement. I'm offered a three year apprenticeship at the Army Apprentices College, near Chepstow in Monmouthshire. If by chance I'm successful, I will become a Corporal Ammunition Technician in the Royal Army Ordnance

Corps. Portability of a job to civilian life as an imperative goes out the window!

At first, my dad isn't impressed. He thinks the RAF would have been a better bet, but he soon comes round and my parents and I sign on the dotted line.

I'm elated. I'd now taken the first big step out of the constraints of one's adolescent environment onto a pathway towards life's big adventures. But it's a step in a direction on which the only real information I have to hand is based on my dad's time in the army, the many war films I'd watched and the *Commando* magazines I hoarded.

I had enjoyed my short time at the ICI, but now I had other things to do.

ARMY APPRENTICE COLLEGE CHEPSTOW — 1967–70

On the day I leave home my dad gives me a little advice.

'Look son, officers may be senior to you, but don't ever think they are better than you.'

I think his advice is actually a philosophy on life. Nobody is better than anyone else; it's just that everyone starts in a different place.

Bushy haired and spotty faced, I step down from the train at Chepstow Railway Station into the mid-afternoon sun on the 4th May 1967, as do a further ten or twenty youths of a similar age. All are part of the May 1967 intake that totals about 120 apprentices and who will forever be known as Group 67B (the second intake of 1967). Every ex-apprentice has a similar label engrained on his heart.

The Army Apprentice College is at Beachley, near Chepstow, situated as it is on the Welsh border at Beachley Point: a peninsula between two rivers – the Severn and Wye. It's home to about 800 apprentices from the age of sixteen to nineteen, and has been since just after the war. Primarily, it is a Royal Engineers college and three quarters of the apprentices will become Royal Engineers. All those guys will leave here to become combat engineers. For now, it's a completely disparate group of eager youths hailing from a variety of backgrounds who know little about military things, but are destined to become men and an integral part of the most professional *green machine* in the world. We can expect to be subject to both a modified Queen's Regulations and Manual of Military Law, but, to all intents and purposes, it is the Army.

Apprentices have their own rank structure, from the lowest rank of apprentice to lance corporal, through to regimental sergeant major. But behind the regimental veneer there also exists an underground public school-type hierarchy based on how long a person has been at the college. Everyone junior to you is called a pig, which is as insulting as it sounds, but stands for 'Passing-in Group'. Despite any lofty rank you might attain at the college, due consideration still had to be taken of this hierarchical pecking order. To step out of line could be to find yourself the focus of attention by a more senior group and this was not a good place to be! The only consolation is that whatever bad things happened to you, well, if you were of a mind to, you could always inflict similar on a group junior to yourself.

11

If you thought this was a form of institutionalised bullying, you would be right.

As we arrive at the college we see a small group of youths climb into the back of a Land Rover. We're told they're being expelled from the college for bullying and extortion. Such things aren't tolerated by the powers that be, but, nonetheless, a form of bullying is ongoing in the guise of public school 'fagging'. Juniors would clean the rooms, run errands and maintain the uniforms of Seniors. It is part of the levelling and building process that would ultimately instil a confidence and *esprit de corps* in you and your mates; by the time you passed out from the college you knew your place, but also the pecking order and, importantly, where the privileges reside – a kind of 'Eton effect', as it might be described.

All that is in the future. For now, we're grouped up according to our respective trades and I get to meet the rest of my Ammo Tech course. There's George Ferguson from a military family, half Irish and with a brother already at the college; Des Kerr from Leicester; Keith Proctor from Croydon; Charles Allen, all the way from Thurso in Scotland, and who speaks in an unintelligible manner; Barry Johnson from Stony Stratford in Bucks, and two other guys who find the pace of the course not to their liking and disappear in quick succession. Two years down the line we would be joined by Ron Strafford when he's back-squadded from a more senior group due to a short illness. We become an entity – a team.

In the bowels of Beachley Camp is Department 22. This is a Royal Army Ordnance Corps oasis. It's the self-contained Ammunition Technician's Department where I will learn the intricacies and the hazards of ammunition and explosives. The department comprises a number of classrooms, together with separate stores where all the ammunition-related equipment is maintained. Some distance away is an Ammunition Process Building used for inspecting and repairing ammunition and which can also be used as a classroom. A fenced and earthed up explosive storehouse is where live examples of ammunition are kept on which we will test our knowledge and practice our skills.

Ammunition Technicians, up until a short time before, had been called Ammunition Examiners and this handle probably better defined the job during the fifties and early sixties. As the job title had now changed so too had the type and scope of the work, but the extent of this was not yet appreciated and Northern Ireland had yet to kick off.

Two notable civilians work at the department; they are Mr Montagu Munday, the storeman – or Monty, as we call him – and Mr Les Gunningham, or 'Gungy' for short. Potential Ammo Techs have for many years benefited from Monty's wise advice and commitment to quality; he's held in high esteem by all the apprentices. Monty is the only civilian I'm aware of to be made an

Getting it together, at last, at the end of the first term; 12 weeks into the apprenticeship.

Outside of Department 22. Early days in the 67B Ammo Tech Course.

honorary Ammunition Technician. Mr Gunningham is an ex-Ammo Tech who settled in the area and became a civilian instructor. He is very enthusiastic and knowledgeable about such things as the theory of obturation and the history of artillery explodering systems. His catchphrase at the end of most sentences always got our course into hysterics: 'Got that, right?' He probably came away thinking we'd all gone mad!

Various trades are grouped up to form platoons and ours is overseen by Sergeant Lyle who is a regular soldier, about thirty-seven years old and from the cavalry. He becomes the regimental father and mother you hear about. From here on in, our lives are in the hands of the tried and well tested military system. This begins with a very short-back-and-sides hair cut and then basic training, which is more about broom handling than weapon handling. We're ground down to basics. To start with we're issued with berets, gaiters, thick scratchy serge trousers left over from the Second World War (or perhaps even the first), equally scratchy shirts and hard leather boots that we polish until we can count our teeth in the reflection. We spend hours and hours cleaning toilets and floors and it is a pleasure to get out and sweep the roads that I had vowed to avoid. We learn to look after ourselves, press shirts and uniforms with razor creases, blanco webbed belts, Brasso the brasses; we get shouted at, square bashed and we learn all the basic drills. I don't think we saw a rifle once in those early weeks. There simply wasn't the time!

The college hierarchy is made up of permanent staff of both the military and civilian types. The military are found from many different areas of the regular army. Trade and educational training is supported by civilian instructors. The Regimental Sergeant Major is always a Guardsman of the archetypical National Service type and a sense of fear precedes his very presence. Members of Corps, as opposed to Regiments, are not generally noted for their drill and turnout skills, so I don't know how he copes with the plethora of different cap badges and their own traditions. Behind the scenes one can imagine it gets occasionally tense and we would sometimes hear such grumblings from our trade instructors. These instructors were Ammunition Technicians and the people we really looked up to.

I think I've already indicated that I am not especially academic and so learning is a real slog for me. It's intensive, and trade tests come at an alarming rate. The pass mark for every exam is 65%; more than two failures in succession and you're off the course! Most exams are a combination of theory and reference, where the latter is to demonstrate your ability to find information from the smallest clue within an enormous pile of reference books (Ammunition and Explosive Regulations).

A third of our time at the college is spent improving our education mainly to get us through the army educational exams that are required to qualify regular soldiers for promotion. There are two levels we have to worry about: the Intermediate and then the Senior Exam, which is probably the equivalent of an O-level. Shortly after arriving we all take a series of tests to measure our academic abilities so that we can be streamed. I find myself placed in level 5 for

Me in situ buried by Ammunition and Explosive Regulations. These expanded exponentially as more guided weapons were introduced and computing became the heart of ammunition quality surveillance.

maths: the lowest group. At our first maths lesson the teacher, Mr Robinson, a Welsh chap, raises himself up and surveys the class over his specs.

'Wharton, where are you boy?'

I put my hand up.

He looks at me. 'Wharton,' he says with his fine, deep Welsh lilt, 'I have never had an Ammunition Technician in my class before.'

Once again it is embarrassing being singled out and, yes, he is also dead right to make a point of it because a light comes on! It's like having a flare set off in my face. My squandered school years are laid bare in front of me. From that point on, I stop being in denial. I am behind the curve and I am to blame. Later that evening I consider my predicament and I feel a panic well up inside me. I desperately want to become an Ammunition Technician and know I will only get one chance at it. I conclude there and then that I can and will do better. The panic, more or less, subsides. A consequence of all this is that I will, pretty much, spend the next three years swotting, incarcerated in the college, only really seeing the light of day when allowed home on block leave.

Not that we have much money to throw about. In 1967 an apprentice's pay starts at £3.50p a week, of which I am allowed to draw £1.50. It buys a couple of packets of fags, a few bars of chocolate and then it is gone. The remainder of my pay is saved for me, accumulated, and handed back on the day I proceed on block leave.

At the end of the first term we officially 'Pass In' to the college with a small parade and a lunch to which our parents are invited. Parents are invited to view the trade training departments. Warrant Officer Class 1 Peter Gurney is the Senior Ammunition Technician at Department 22 and he shows my parents around the ammunition museum. At this point there's still no sign or mention of the improvised explosive devices that would occupy the profession in the coming years. Peter Gurney would eventually become an expert in that specialist field and make his name as the head of the Metropolitan Police Bomb Squad during the seventies and eighties.

Afterwards, my family and I catch the train back to Poulton-le-Fylde. There's a long way to go in terms of training, but I'm already buoyed up by the realisation that I'm part of something that I enjoy and have been accepted and have accepted the regimental ethos. Once accepting it, any soldier will tell you, you never lose it.

I've been handed my accumulated pay, which amounts to about £30. In 1967 it's more money than I had even seen before. Sadly, it is quickly frittered away on Blackpool's golden mile and Pleasure Beach. Later, there would be ample opportunities to spend it on beer and wild women but, even so, much of it would still get squandered.

As the first year progresses we read in the newspapers of rioting in Hong Kong, as leftists and Communists try to destabilise that province. We hear that an Ammunition Technician, an ex-Beachley boy, Charles Workman, has been killed there trying to defuse a bomb. It comes as a bit of a shock, but information about the incident is sketchy and we are always aware that Ammo Tech work can be risky. The real significance of that unusual incident in that very foreign and seemingly remote place pretty much escapes all of us.

I put my back into the maths course. I'm able to recall the maths techniques and layout protocols I'd been taught at secondary school, but this time around I'm listening to the teacher, and the subject matter actually begins to make sense. At the end of the first term I pass the Intermediate level maths exam and by the end of the sixth term I pass the Senior exam and don't have to take maths again. I amazed myself!

The months and years pass at the college and I'm steadily promoted up the apprentice ladder, eventually reaching the lofty rank of sergeant. Others receive similar promotions, but it's George Ferguson who becomes the apprentice regimental sergeant major.

Regimental and physical training take up a third of our time at the college. Parades come thick and fast, but it's the Queen's official birthday parade that sticks in the mind. It's not a lot of fun. We dread it, coming as it does in the middle of summer; the weather is always hot or red hot. Because many dignitaries are invited to the final spectacle it requires a number of practices and even a full dress rehearsal. Accompanied by the bands, we are all marched onto the square and then stood at ease. Then we are left to stand. Time passes as the sun beats down onto the baking tarmac. First your hat seems to get heavier and heavier. It presses down on your temples. You feel sweat drip down your cheek off your chin. Your head begins to ache and your eyes begin to swim. The Commandant's podium appears to wobble in the heat haze. At least twenty minutes of silence has probably passed when I hear the first thud. A minute or so later I hear another. Out of the corner of my eye I can see a guy to my right as he begins to buckle at the knees. He sinks to the ground in a heap. Others are not quite that lucky and crash forward or backward, as if they've been struck by a mallet. All around me, bodies thud to the ground. As each guy faints, orderlies (stood by for this event) rush out from the sidelines and, with what can only be mischievous intent, drag each lad to the side of the square ensuring that all the polish on his toe caps is scraped off by the asphalt.

Relief eventually arrives in the shape of the rotund Commandant and his two pristine orderlies. We hear their boots crunching on the gravel behind us as they march down from the Commandant's quarters. He takes his place at the podium ready for the march past and the salute. When we are brought to

Looking useful in the Dept 22 Explosive Storehouse. Actually I'm posing for an army recruiting photograph. Note the seriously scratchy serge trousers which brought many a lad out in a rash.

attention, just moving the body brings great relief.

In 1968, I counted at least twenty lads who fainted at the rehearsal. This was not seen as a failing of the system in any way, but a general lack of moral fibre in the lads. We are, therefore, roused from our beds at 5 a.m. on the morning of Her Majesty's parade and marched down to the open air swimming pool for a dip to wake us up. And it certainly does.

The Ammo Tech trade training is hard work but extremely interesting and, slowly and surely, the ammunition world begins to reveal itself to me. There are so many different weapon systems, each with a different purpose and history. Within each there are different types of ammunition, within each type there are different model numbers – each has its own idiosyncrasies and terminologies, and they are all colour coded.

All have different fuzing systems, differing hazards, storage and handling requirements, proof requirements, inspection and test needs and disposal methods. There is a multitude of inspection and repair equipment.

I quickly learn that, at the end of their shelf life, ammunition and explosives have to be got rid of safely. Even at the very end they have a bite and are very unforgiving if you treat them wrongly. It soon becomes clear that, as an Ammunition Technician, I need to recognise and understand all these things and all of the risks associated with them. Gradually, I learn the vocabulary and the environment takes shape.

It's probably obvious, but the quality of ammunition, unlike wine, doesn't get better as the years roll on and the shelf life for some natures can be at least twenty years. Soldiers at the sharp end in battle, however, don't often get a second chance if the stuff doesn't work correctly. Quality is, therefore, key. The title 'Technician' might be considered close to that of an 'Engineer', so an Ammo Tech's overriding day job is engineering this changing quality throughout its shelf life.

During the eighties, the British Army had worldwide stocks worth about £2bn. Admittedly, this is a value that isn't simple to explain, since the questions it raises are: is this the original cost to buy it or the cost to replace it many years later? Do the costs include its packaging and what about the overall cost of storing and maintaining it? Everyone is probably guessing at what the real value is. Nonetheless, it gives an idea of scale for a commodity that (even MoD bean counters will agree) has idiosyncrasies, which are different to manage to, say, vehicles or spanners.

Northern Ireland kicks off with a vengeance in 1969. Night after night, we all sit in front of the communal TV screen, transfixed, as the rioting and violence grows out of all proportion. Finally, the army is called in, but instead of solving the problem the rioting turns to shooting and worse is just around the corner.

**Successful students and Instructors of the 67B Ammo Tech course. I'm on the right of the picture, front row.
Behind me is Gus Garside, an Instructor who 5 years down the line will not return from the Long Walk.**

In the final year at the college, having passed all the education exams, I bump into my ex-maths teacher, Mr Robinson. He looks pleased to see me.

'Wharton,' he says, calling me over in that rich Welsh tone. 'Do you know, boy, you were my star pupil?'

I'm taken aback by this. He goes on, 'I still have your exercise book. I've used it ever since to show my students how I expect them to present their work.'

I blush profusely.

Mr Saxon, my maths teacher at Hodgson School, might finally have been proud of me – and completely gobsmacked!

Trade exam follows exam. I hang in there and eventually I scrape through the course. I'm placed sixth out of a course of seven, but I qualified. It's a big relief. I think a pass is the only real yard stick by which to measure these things. After that it's how you perform and apply the knowledge, isn't it?

One of the final regimental tests we have to get through is a forced march called the 'ten mile bash'. All apprentices have to demonstrate that they've achieved what is a 'teeth arms', i.e. infantry standard of fitness. It's the culmination of three years' fitness training. In full kit and boots, together with a rifle and a pack on our backs, we have to march and run 10 miles in one hour forty minutes. This timing doesn't appear to make any allowances for the hills, which on any other occasion make the area look so pretty.

It's a hot day as we quick-march out of the college and then break into a run. 'Left, right, left, right, left, right!' the PT Instructor shouts and the squad gets into its rhythm. Anyone around the corner would think a steam engine was approaching. After a few miles we are conscious of equipment banging against our hips, the rifle strap rubbing our shoulders sore and our feet blistering. The soldiers all around are steaming. After 8 miles or so, we feel the pain in our sides, our lungs are bursting and it takes a grim determination not to give up. It's hard not to feel extremely irritated with the guy in front, who has lost the step and is upsetting the rhythm.

Even with our level of fitness it's still a shock to the system. After one hour and thirty minutes on the road we're back and, with the stronger guys helping the weaker, everyone gets through. Then, without any rest, we complete the rest of the test. I pick up a mate in a fireman's lift and carry him the regulatory 50 yards before dropping him like a brick. I then run at, and haul myself over, a 6-foot wall with my rifle. After that, I'm finally finished, in more ways than one. Wearily, I stagger back to the barrack block to nurse my blisters and bruises. I'm burning up, so hot it feels like I'll ignite. I decide to have a cold bath – big mistake. It causes my stomach to spasm and I vomit across the floor.

In May 1970, we finally Pass Out from the college. The Passing Out parade is a whole college event unlike the Passing In parade. All 800 apprentices are

1970. - The Senior Group 'march past' during the Passing Out Parade. Ron Strafford is 2nd along in the front row, I'm third, Barry Johnson is 7th and Keith Proctor is out the front about to give the order to turn.

Right: The Apprentice College Gate at Beachley. All that remains today of an institution that brought life skills, pride and discipline to thousands of young lads.

on parade. It's quite spectacular, attended, as it is, by lots of parents and many dignitaries from far and wide. It ends with the three bands playing 'Auld Lang Syne' as we, the Senior Group, slow-march through the funnel formed by the remainder of the apprentices.

The parade brings to an end three years of a grinding, refining and then honing process on which, despite its ups and downs, I will always look back with affection. We were all young men ready to take on the world. Smart, possibly over confident, as fit in body as we would ever be and with a personal pride that burst out of our chests.

The army doesn't provide this type of apprenticeship any more or even a boy service as such. It's all gone into the ether. The scheme was ended in the eighties. Too costly, I guess, or was it a political response to criticism that the young men of the UK were being compared to the young men we see in the armies of Africa? I don't know. Beachley is now an ordinary army camp for regular soldiers, with only the Beachley Camp gates preserved. What I do know is that it was a superb institution that picked up thousands of aimless young men and placed them on the road to something better. Forget 'boot camps'; this system provided education and quality training in a variety of work skills. It will never be bettered by any other system. Those who are interested in such things might take notice.

At the prize-giving that follows I am awarded the trophy for the best rifle shot in the college. Well, I wasn't going to win any prizes for academics, was I? And, in any case, as I liked to tell people, no enemy soldier was ever killed by a well answered maths or chemistry paper!

On leaving the college new Ammunition Technicians are immediately promoted to regular army full corporals. A big step frankly, and this hike up the ladder from nowhere is pretty much resented throughout our own corps. The only way to counter the criticism is to grow up quickly and act like a full corporal. However, I am still only nineteen years old and it would be a mistake to think that the army is all that occupies my mind at this time!

The training is not yet over, however – oh no. Ammo Techs are now sent to the RAOC Depot at Blackdown near Camberley for a three week regimental course. This will provide us with the regimental-type qualifications that befit a corporal in the regular army.

The training starts badly when we all turn up a day late, but I think the instructors are ultimately taken aback and impressed by our abilities; there is no doubt that we are very capable in terms of our fitness, drill, turnout and weapon handling. Well we'd already had three years of moulding into the right shape.

After this, it is onward and upward to the Army School of Ammunition, which, at this time, is part of the Central Ammunition Depot located near the little village of Bramley in Hampshire. The Army School of Ammunition is the army's centre of competence for all ammunition-related courses. It also takes serving soldiers from any area of the army who want to become Ammunition Technicians. If successful, they transfer into the profession from their regiment or corps. This is effectively the adult entry route. The course has similar technical content to the apprenticeship, but, without the regimental or educational elements, the duration of their course is reduced by two-thirds. Commissioned RAOC officers who require the ammunition specialisation are also trained in this way. They are also required to attend, as a precursor, an explosive science-related module at the Royal Military College of Science at Shrivenham.

For obvious reasons, ammo depots are always sited a long way from towns, so they are often in the most picturesque parts of the country. In this respect, Bramley is great. What is not so great is the ten-week modular course on guided weapon systems, which I now have to pass. This course encompasses surface to air, ground to ground and helicopter to surface missile systems. Each system is unique with its own distinct control systems, guidance systems, payloads, render safe mechanisms, safety in arming, ground equipments, etc, etc. Coming, as it does, on top of the previous three years is extremely tough, and I only manage to scrape through this lot by the skin of my teeth. Even then I'm hauled in front of the chief instructor and read the riot act for not trying hard enough. This criticism isn't easy to accept, since I am trying as hard as I bloody well can!

Following the Guided Weapons course we are briefly introduced to the art and science behind terrorist devices. It's a one week course that introduces us to the 'empire' techniques of bomb disposal. This must be one of the last bomb disposal courses of its type and I will touch on the types of things we were taught later in the book.

In the summer of 1970, one year after troops were deployed on the streets of Ulster, we finally arrive at the end of the 'Ammunition Technician sausage machine' and we are ready to take our place within the big green fighting machine. Unbeknown to us, though, the Ammo Tech profession is grimly facing up to its biggest challenge.

The postings come through; some of us are posted to the British Army of the Rhine (BAOR) and some will remain in the UK. Kerr gets posted to the Ammunition Sub Depot at Ballykinler in Ulster; Proctor and Johnson go to the Central Ammunition Depot at Kineton in Warwickshire; Allen and Ferguson go to 154 Forward Ammunition Depot at Wulfen in West Germany, and Strafford and I are also off to Germany, but to 3 Base Ammunition and Petroleum Depot, near Monchengladbach. Separated at this point, we never served together again as one entity, but the group ethos runs deep and we have all remained good friends from then, even until today.

JUNIOR AMMO TECH
1970–74

The unit 3 BAPD is located near the little village of Bracht, outside Monchengladbach. In 1970, the depot spans at least 50 square miles of real estate and is, therefore, one of the largest ammunition depots of its kind in Europe. The land is mainly conifer forest with a myriad of dusty tracks that disappear off into the trees from the larger roads laid with tarmac. Many ammunition locations are simple corrugated iron shelters, which have been temporary since the Second World War. Other locations are new, much larger and built of brick and concrete to house the hundreds of thousands of newly palletised ammunition boxes.

Deer live in the depot and a blood-sucking horsefly, which soldiers call a 'cleg', follows them around. This is a thoroughly nasty bastard of an insect. Unlike a wasp, which flies around your head making up its mind, the cleg comes straight in without warning. A large weal on the arm or neck is the first telltale signs that you've been attacked. If you have the misfortune to be allergic to it, God help you. It makes some areas of the depot a misery to work in and I've never come across anything quite like that bloody cleg anywhere else.

The western edge of the depot nestles up against the Dutch border; in fact, this is as far west as you can get in Germany. This makes perfect sense, as the Soviet Bloc tanks would have to traverse the full length of Germany to reach us, leaving us time to out-load the ammunition to those who would have to use it for real. Having said that, the out-load strategy really relies on a period of increasing tension before hostilities finally break out. Whether we would have got it will never been known. My guess is that the outbreak of that war would have been more like Pearl Harbour, since (taking purely a military standpoint) it's the only invasion strategy that really made sense.

Ron and I arrive at the unit late at night. We are already aware that 3 BAPD has a reputation that precedes it – it is seen by the troops as a punishment posting! We'd flown in earlier that day, but had been left in the bar at RAF Wildenrath all afternoon and evening, since no transport had been organised to collect us. By the time I arrive at the camp I'm pretty much the worse for wear. Not having had much drinking practice at the college, I had still to perfect the art. I spend my first night in a spare bed in one of the barrack blocks.

In the morning, I awake and look around me at the four grey walls that surround me and I realise that I am not, in fact, dreaming. To say that there's been a lack of investment in the place would be an understatement and it's not hard to see why soldiers might think they had done something wrong to be posted here. Damp is evident in the plaster on both the ceilings and walls. The paintwork is battered and chipped and the floors are covered in a 'gopping' cardinal-red polish that contaminates and stains everything that touches it. These are the first things I see, so it's pretty depressing – a real 'oh my God!' moment.

The following year there is some investment in the place and the barrack blocks are refurbished (monies left over from the depot explosive area rebuild, I guess). Even an open air swimming pool is built, but, for some reason or other, a barbed wire fence is immediately erected around it and it is never used. The beginnings of 'elf and safety' I suspect.

By dint of a strange coincidence, there are five soldiers in the unit called Brown. Each has a different nickname: Nosher, Knocker, Topper, Bomber and Charlie (of course). Also by dint of an equally strange coincidence, each is awaiting a Court Marshal for a different prevalent offence. You couldn't make it up!

Serving here is nothing like Chepstow. At Chepstow, reveille was at 6.30 a.m. and lights out at 10.30 p.m. but here things are much more relaxed. Soldiers are free to get up at whatever time they want providing they get to work on time. A muster parade is held just once a week. Weekends are free time unless you're required for a duty. Each morning, soldiers stream out of the barrack blocks chatting and laughing, making their way either to their cars with their distinctive British Forces number plates or, if not, to the large military trucks belching fumes that wait to convey them to their places of work within the Depot Explosives Area.

In the evening, many soldiers just retire to the NAAFI bar and this is their tedious routine for the two or three years they're posted here.

The married quarters are about 2 miles away at Op De Haag, the other side of Bracht village. The 'pads', as they're called, amuse themselves with parties that we young soldiers only get to fantasise about!

Across from the Depot Administrative Area is a separate camp of wooden huts where hundreds of Portuguese labourers live. Soldiers call them 'pork and cheese'. They provide the labour to move around the vast quantity of loose ammunition containers. This will end shortly when ammunition is fully palletised, but, for now, much of it has to be shifted by hand.

Alongside the labour camp live the MSO. These are the dog handlers who guard the depot at night. Mainly Poles, they are classified as misplaced persons having left Poland as the Russians arrived there in 1945, unable to return. It can't be much fun for them.

Time motors on and I slip into the various routines. Duties are a fact of life in the army and corporals are periodically required to carry out a duty as Guard Commander. The duty is performed from the guardroom and mainly revolves around trying to keep a lid on the place during silent hours. At this time, the Black September Arab terrorist group is making a nuisance of itself in Europe and PIRA are still establishing themselves in Ulster, but, frankly, they are the least of my problems. The main issues arise from the occupants within the camp rather than without. On one occasion, as my duty driver leaves the guardroom, a drunken soldier nuts him, just for the hell of it. Arresting the perpetrator from the protection of his equally drunken mates is not easy. On another occasion, a Glaswegian soldier wrecks a barrack room and, after we arrest him, manages to dive through the serving hatch, which is no mean feat considering the size of him. He then smashes up the guardroom. The Orderly Officer arrives, disgruntled because he's been called from the mess bar, and verbally berates the prisoner. Not a good idea. The guy then goes for the Orderly Officer and pushes him out of the way before trying to escape. I see this coming and deploy my guards to tactical positions either side of the door making it much easier to ambush and throttle him as he charges at us! Thrown bodily back into the cell, the door slammed after him, he is left to sleep it off on a cold wooden bench. Not giving him a cup of tea in the morning, however, would probably have got me arrested these days.

It is around this time that a fellow Ammo Tech has the misfortune of being Guard Commander when a member of his own guard tries to shoot himself! The guy manages to get a poorly aimed shot off before he is disarmed. 'Events' are a regular occurrence, so duties are never boring. There are many things about 3 BAPD that are unlike any other unit I will ever serve with.

The Unit's main salvation is, undoubtedly, its proximity to the English-speaking Dutch towns of Venlo, Roermond and also Echt. They become happy hunting grounds for those of us looking for a bit of fun. And, when you're a young soldier, this is what life seems to be all about. In fact, I am informed by the owners of one Dutch discotheque that the British Army's contribution, in terms of beer purchased, is the only thing that keeps the place afloat! We make a lot of friends there and many guys have Dutch girlfriends. Some even marry them. All it takes is a nod and a wink to the guy on guard and you can smuggle a girl into camp.

As my time at 3 BAPD continues, I join the shooting team and meet Sergeant Alan Glasby, also an Ammo Tech. He becomes my shooting mentor. To become a top class rifle shot you need nerves of steel since any hand shake is immediately transferred to the weapon. Alan has this, but, alas, I do not. So, whilst I will win a number of competitions and trophies over the coming years,

I will never attain anything like his standard. In 1971, however, the 3 BAPD shooting team becomes a force to be reckoned with and the team to beat.

Alan had already made a name for himself as a Queen's medallist, becoming the best rifle shot in the entire British Army – not bad going for a corporal in the Royal Army Ordnance Corps. Alan would go on to even greater things in competition shooting and was awarded the OBE and the George Medal for operationally related matters. He eventually left the army as a Lt Colonel, having become an exceptional, self-taught wood sculptor. Then, only in his early sixties, he was taken by cancer. Alan Glasby was probably the most gifted and talented person I ever knew. I was able to tell him this a day or so before he died. It is hard to believe, even now, that he has passed.

Within the ammo depot, most Ammunition Technicians are employed in the Ammunition Process Area. German civilians assist us and the depot is a major employer in the area. Some speak English and they are happy to tell us of their time during the war. Those who were captured by the Russians were often put to work in the salt mines, not being freed until years after the war ended. No one owns up to supporting Herr Adolf, but then, who would?

Our job is to inspect random samples selected from the complete range of ammunition natures that is brought into the Ammunition Process Building. The Ammo Techs inspect them for defects and signs of deterioration. Sometimes entire model numbers and whole batches have to be repaired. The latter work can be more hazardous because, despite precise instructions, there is always the tendency to push things along more speedily or bend the rules. If people do this, they increase the risks. It is down to supervisors to ensure everyone works safely, but, unfortunately, some don't always rise to the occasion and, therefore, incidents occur overtime. Occasionally, people get injured or even die.

Hazards are everywhere and some are not always entirely obvious. For example, at this time, the military use nitro glycerine-based (NG) demolition explosives manufactured by ICI. It's light green with a consistency of malleable wax. During a routine inspection, I make the mistake of not wearing protective gloves. Such things aren't easy to come by in any case. The trouble with NG is that it is absorbed through the pores of the skin and this gives a person a migraine-type headache, which, in some quarters, is called 'NG head'. I find out this idiosyncrasy the hard way. It's seen as a bit of a joke by the hierarchy – a sort of induction event. I'm bedded down for a whole day! Making mistakes in this job, either out of ignorance or sloppiness, always tends to have repercussions one way or another.

In order for us to gain maximum work experience, we're routinely rotated through the different work areas, spending a few weeks in one job before being moved on. The more practical jobs that involve a bit of flash, bang, wallop, tend to be the most interesting. For example the Proof Centre sited in the middle of the complex enables explosives to be tested and ammunition components to be proof fired. This is good, but easily the best place to be assigned is the demolition ground or, as the Germans have it, *Der Sprengplatz*.

Every ammunition depot has a similar area set aside whereby small quantities of ammunition can be disposed of, usually by burning or demolition. If you live near an ammunition depot you will know this because, when the cloud level is low, the shock waves of an explosion will actually bounce off and rattle or even, on occasion, break your windows!

At 3 BAPD, the 'dem' ground is deep in the forest, some distance from civilisation and just short of where the perimeter fence is also the Dutch border. For the incautious or reckless, it is a veritable Aladdin's cave. In terms of danger, it has the potential to be right up there with the warring streets of Belfast. Alcoholism affects a lot of British soldiers in Germany. The culture has always tacitly supported the excessive drinking and years of tax free, cheap booze have taken a toll on many. My unit has its share of alcoholics. I work for a Staff Sergeant Ammo Tech (let's call him IM); by the afternoon he is always the worse for wear and reeks of booze. If you had an alcoholic Staff Sergeant Ammo Tech on your books where would you avoid employing him? Everywhere? Well, he's in charge of the demolition ground and I'm his 'gopher'. I need explain no further; the implications are obvious.

A common reason for the disposal of ammunition is when the British Army change to a new artillery piece (for example, when we changed from the 5.5 inch Howitzer to the 155mm self-propelled gun); the former became defunct, together with its vast stocks of ammunition. The powers-that-be tried to sell the whole weapon system to another country, but, this was not possible, so it is our job to destroy the ammunition. On this occasion, we find ourselves with a hundred thousand large cordite propelling charges to be disposed of. One way of disposing of them is to lay out 15,000kg worth of cartridges at a time and then ignite them. This work is considered hazardous and, in the past, people have been killed carrying it out.

Therefore 3 BAPD has what is called a Semi-Continuous Burning Plant, designed to dispose of unwanted artillery propelling charges more safely. It's a small brick building atop a slope and in one room, the propelling charges of about 5kg of cordite – with their integral bright red (and very spark sensitive) gunpowder igniters – are unpacked from their waxed cardboard tubes. The charges are then passed through a hatch to an Ammo Tech in a second room. By using a mirror to ensure the metal slide outside is clear, he pops the charge through a rotating hatch where it falls nicely onto the slide and slips neatly down it into a fire at the bottom of the slope. There, it is immediately consumed with a whoosh of white hot heat. The operation is slow and tedious, since the operating instructions say that only one charge can be dealt with at a time. When you have thousands of these to get rid of there is always going to be a temptation, for some anyway, to short cut the system.

As you will imagine, there are procedures for everything on a dem ground, but such procedures are obviously only going to be useful if they are followed. Returning to our SSgt IM, he does not tend to go by the book. For example, he has his own technique for running a SCBP, which is to pile six or seven unpacked propelling charges onto the arms, take them out through the door, make his way round the building to the slide, drop the charges onto the slide, one after the other, stand back and watch the volcano. This method was working quite efficiently until, one day, his technique almost did for him. And far worse – nearly did for me!

'Corporal Wharton,' he yells. 'Come here, laddie. You've just completed the course haven't you? What do you make of these?'

He passes me an olive drab metal tube and I turn it over in my hands. It's about 75cm long with a 30mm diameter. It's open at one end, from which a crumbling powder is apparent. Unfortunately, there are no markings on it that would answer the question for him.

'Dunno, Staff. It doesn't seem to have a fuze though. Is there any documentation with it?'

'F**cking useless,' he says. 'Give it here.'

Snatching the metal object back, he places it into one of the cardboard tubes and, walking over to the SCBP, he drops it onto the metal slide. We watch the tube accelerate down the slope into the inferno at the bottom. With, I have to say, some trepidation on my part, we await events. Nothing happens.

'Must be inert,' he mutters under his breath. 'Come on, back to work, laddie.'

He pushes me into the SCBP and, still in a hurry, takes another pile of charges in both arms and disappears out of the building. All of a sudden I hear a strange shrieking sound, akin to a jet engine at full thrust, and I mentally calculate that Staff Sgt IM has just had enough time to get around the building to the metal slide. Fearing the worst, I open the door and look out, just as a 'pork and cheese' runs past, heading in the opposite direction. People running on a demolition ground is always a bad sign.

I quickly move round the outside of the building, but pull up sharp when I arrive alongside Staff Sgt IM. His hands are full of the spark-sensitive cordite charges and he's swaying from side to side, trying to balance them. He's swaying because he's trying to predict the path of the anonymous metal item, which we now know to be some kind of a rocket. Veering to and fro, it is effectively hovering above the pit, about 15ft above the ground. The flaming 'flux' from the business end is emitting the jet-like scream. Unstable and unsure, the rocket seems to be trying to decide on a direction of travel. Meanwhile, one spark into his arms and Staff Sgt IM will be Guy Fawkes.

Seeing no point in both of us going the same way, I begin to move backwards, ever quicker, until I come up against the building. Before I can think of a better evasive action, the rocket makes up its mind and, with a Wroooom! that completely drowns out IM's strangled cries, it takes off into the blue yonder. Away it goes, up and up, over the trees, away from the two of us. In a second, all that's left is a bendy trail of blue smoke slowly dispersing in the afternoon sunshine. It occurs to me that it is heading directly for the Company Headquarters, but the big question of 'where did the bloody thing land?' is never answered, which, I guess, is just as well since it could have either set the depot on fire or knocked someone's brains out. It's probably still out there today, embedded in a tree, deep in the forest. Please let me know if you find it.

Now on his knees, but unscathed, and with his arms still full, Staff Sgt IM climbs to his feet as German and Portuguese labourers begin to appear from where they'd taken cover. Smiling, and with just a little embarrassment, he states in his ripe Aberdeen accent the bleedin' obvious. 'Aye well, perhaps I could have dealt with that a little differently.'

The incident was never reported, so Staff Sgt IM lived to abuse another day. Should I have reported this? Probably, but I was young.

Had Staff Sgt IM learned a lesson by this? Well, no. A couple of weeks later we are disposing of White Phosphorous grenades. WP is not an item to mess around with. White Phosphorous grenades are used to provide instantaneous and dense clouds of white smoke with which to obscure things. Infantry and tanks use them to hide their position, enabling them to approach the enemy or even to escape from a sticky situation. WP, the chemical, is a dreadful thing if it should land on the skin; as long as air can get to it, it will burn.

At 3 BAPD we have a local, if apparently questionable, dispensation to burn unserviceable and unwanted grenades in an incinerator. Similar to the SCBP, this method also involves a metal slide with a burning area at the bottom of a slope. But it does not have a brick building attached. Instead, the operative works from a wriggly tin shelter placed precariously at the top of the slope, which is more to keep the rain off than anything else. The idea is that a grenade, without its detonator, is dropped down the slide and enters the fire pit at the bottom of the slope. It quickly heats up and the casing ruptures. As air gets to the WP, it ignites with a big poof of white smoke. Once this event has occurred, another can be sent down. Again, the work is slow and monotonous and, therefore, much too tedious for Staff Sgt IM. He opens a grenade container, takes a handful of prepared grenades and, pushing me out of the way, drops them all (perhaps five or six) down the chute one after the other. After some minutes of nothing happening, I look around the corner of the wriggly tin shelter just as there is a big bang and a tremendous whoosh. All the grenades function simultaneously and I'm looking at a wall of white phosphorous hurtling up the chute towards me. With a cry, I throw myself back just in time, as the wall of phos' reaches the top end of the slide and shoots past the wriggly tin shelter. Staff Sgt IM nearly wets himself laughing. I don't entirely share the joke.

Other incidents occur over time, which I also survive. Another example would be Staff Sgt IM's method of disposing of pyrotechnic flares. These flares are like a more powerful version of a roman candle. Standing behind a wall, IM fires them by flicking the switch on the base of the tube and lobbing them over the wall. He does this just as a German labourer and I pass by. The thing pops off and the magnesium flare streaks towards us. I step back and the labourer next to me leaps forward just as the white hot projectile shoots between us, missing us by a couple of inches!

The incidents I've just recounted were undoubtedly reckless because, over time, this type of behaviour claims lives and seriously injures others. The disposal of ammunition and explosives is rightly subject to stringent procedures and woe betide those who ignore them. The mantra is that working to defined procedures is the safest way of dealing with ammunition and explosives. People who step out of line are considered reckless and dealt with accordingly. I agree with all this and I eventually made a career out of ensuring the regulations and procedures were applied such that the inherent risks were reduced. As I became more senior, ensuring people's safety became more and more central to my job.

An habitual cowboy, whether Staff Sgt IM ever got his comeuppance I do not know. Although I suspect it likely that he eventually succumbed to the demon drink.

Throughout my tour in Germany, Ammo Tech losses in Northern Ireland are a regular and almost routine event. In March 1972, the Commanding Officer of the unit there, Major Calladene, is also killed. In my mind, there is still a sense of unreality about it all. I say this mainly because the guys are all much senior to me and I don't know any of them.

Five months later, however, and all the talk at 3 BAPD is around Warrant Officer 'Nobby' Clark: a family man from our unit who I did know personally. He is killed near the village of Clady whilst trying to clear a device in a milk churn. I think I can say, at this point, that the reality of the work finally strikes home.

In February of 1973, I'm posted out of Germany to the Central Ammunition Depot at Kineton in Warwickshire. I'm sorry to leave. I had grown up at 3 BAPD.

Above: The positano yellow Fiat Sport Coupe I learned to drive in. Note the distinctive British Forces number plate that seemed to attract a lot of attention in the UK.

Right: 1972 - 3 BAPD champion shooting team. I'm third from right. Alan Glasby third from left.

My tour in Germany can be summarised thus: significant pay rises, due mainly to the massive inflation running in the UK; a considerable amount of German and Dutch beer consumed; an immeasurable number of duty free cigarettes smoked; a brand new sporty car purchased and then later crashed at Pirbright, Surrey, in a sober daytime skid on wet leaves; at least twenty trophies obtained in shooting competitions; an ongoing battle with my superiors over the length of my moustache and hair, and some great experiences with Dutch girls who behaved like we were the liberating forces their parents had welcomed in 1944.

By the time I arrive back in the UK I'm older, a little senior and, therefore (I like to think), I'm beginning to act more responsibly. Well, by the end of that year I've given up smoking at least.

My posting coincides with me passing the final trade exams that lift me from a Technician class 2 to 1. The only thing now preventing me from being promoted to sergeant is time, since the rank of sergeant is awarded automatically to Ammunition Technicians after five years in the profession. This would be due in 1975. In the meantime I have 1974 to get through.

The alternative way to dispose of artillery Propelling Charges. Lay out 15,000kgs and ignite it. Hazards associated are not to be underestimated.

One great advantage CAD Kineton has over 3 BAPD is that girls are actually on-site. You don't have to go looking for them. A sizeable proportion of the unit are Women's Royal Army Corps. The girls work in the ammunition process area alongside the troops and, needless to say, everyone has a lot of fun. Many marriages are thus made – and perhaps broken. If scandal and gossip are what make you tick, well, there is no shortage of it.

A company of soldiers from the Royal Pioneer Corps are also resident at the unit, primarily for security reasons and to assist the RAOC Supply Specialists, who manage the depot storage area. There's quite a lot of argy-bargy between the two corps, especially between the RPC and the Ammo Techs. The RPC seem to have an embedded view that, because Ammo Techs are paid more, they tend to appeal to the more attractive girls. I always thought it was because we were better looking, but hey ho; this type of friction tends to manifest itself more once people have had a few drinks. During my time here this aggravation doesn't break out into a full blown riot, but it occasionally comes close. Sometimes, rogue elements of the RPC go out of their way to find someone to beat up. They seem to consider it a sport. This is how it was. For example, one evening in Leamington Spa, an Ammo Tech (Corporal PM) has a short altercation with an RPC guy in a chip shop. A short time after, PM is eating his chips whilst peering into a shop window when he sees, reflected in the glass, the same guy approaching him from behind with clear intent. Swivelling around, he kicks out, connects and down the guy goes. Not even spilling a chip, he leaves him groaning on the pavement and goes on his way. After this, the word goes out among the RPC that Corporal PM has to be dealt with.

A few nights later, on his way back to the barrack block from the NAAFI, Corporal PM is confronted by four RPC guys who line up in front of him. Uppermost in their mind is almost certainly the need to redeem the honour of their Corps, not to mention revenge for their colleague's beating. PM wears spectacles and doesn't look like Rocky, so the RPC have probably concluded that he is a soft touch. With their intentions completely obvious, however, before anything concrete has even been said, PM has thumped the first guy, nutted the second and kicked the third in the groin. Bish, bash, bosh! Down they all go. The fourth scarpers. It is hard to feel sorry for a group of men bound on committing grievous bodily harm, but on this occasion I suppose we could. As you will gather, PM is not someone to mess with. To add insult to their injuries, the next day, PM places them all on a charge for assault. I have to say, at the time, we all think that this is the really cool bit!

The particular lesson I expect the RPC took from this is 'know your enemy!'

1ST TOUR NI — 1974

I first got a taste for the tricks of the IEDD business when I attended that short introductory course on bomb disposal in 1970, at the end of the apprenticeship. The course was followed, a couple of years later, by another two-week bomb disposal module, which formed part of the upgrading course that saw me rise from Technician Class 2 to 1. It is only because I'm still effectively qualifying as an Ammunition Technician that I have all these courses to attend. Those who are already beyond Corporal by this time will only get one course, i.e. one bite at the training cherry before they are on the streets of Ulster doing it for real.

Any Ammo Tech who cannot pass these courses will lose his professional qualification and be 're-mustered' into another trade. It's a policy borne out of providing equity for all those who go operational. For the same reason, anyone sent home early from an operational tour, due perhaps to a misdemeanour, could also expect the same treatment. So it wasn't simply a case of staying alive, it also required you to succeed in the eyes of all those you served. I have to say, at the time, I did not consider the latter to be particularly significant. But then I was still young and quite inexperienced.

In late November, 1973, I'm working in the offices at the Ammunition Process Area in Kineton Depot when I'm told by my supervisor, Staff Sgt Graham Crawshaw, that I've been nominated for a tour in Northern Ireland. My time has come. A shiver of excitement runs through me, or maybe it's trepidation. Graham tells me that I'll enjoy it and relates some of his own experiences, by which he had been Mentioned in Despatches (MID). Less than six months later, however, he is tragically killed in an accident on a training area near Liverpool whilst demonstrating IEDs to police forensic scientists. His is the first funeral of its kind I attend. They never get any easier.

At this point, I know for sure that I have, almost by accident, found myself in a career that is arguably going to be one of the more hazardous that people can envisage doing. And, very soon, I would know what it was like at the coal face. Would I measure up? Strangely, my apprehension at this probably outweighs every other concern, even that of dying. It even overrides any concerns I have for the feelings of family and friends. Whether I have the inner wherewithal to do the job is what bothers me the most.

Pre Operations Course - In the back row, far right is Staff Sergeant Lew Bean (No 16). I'm in the middle at the front in the combat kit (No 10). Second from the left in the front row is Sergeant Mick O'Neill (No 4). I'll speak about Lew and Mick later in the book.

In early 1974, I attend an NI Pre-Operations IEDD course, after which I'm told that I will be the No. 2, the Operator's Assistant, on a team that operates out of Omagh. The tour will commence the following April, but before that date is even reached, another Ammo Tech, Staff Sergeant Alan Brammah, doesn't return from the long walk.

Finally, the day arrives and I catch the Liverpool to Belfast ferry along with all other Security Forces embarking for Ulster. Arriving at the Liverpool terminal in amongst a veritable melee of soldiers, I hear my name called out by the Movements staff. I push my way to the front of the throng, thinking how important the work and I must be, being called to the front of the queue. But I'm brought down a peg or two when I'm told to sign for a prisoner who I'm to escort to Belfast. He's an infantry Lance Corporal who's deserted and is being sent back to face retribution. At least I'm given a bunk for the night crossing. There's nowhere for him to run and so the passage is uneventful. He tells me that he can't deal with the pressure any more. Whether that is true or not I'll never know.

On arriving at Belfast docks, four of his colleagues are waiting to take him away and this is my first sight of soldiers on operations. It isn't what I expected. The soldiers look and sound weary, as if they haven't slept for days. Their uniforms are tatty and dusty. Beneath the jacket each wears a sweat shirt rather than the regulation scratchy shirts I'm issued with. Their flack jackets are spattered with paint and torn in places. Their rifles are scratched and wrapped in masking tape with double magazines taped together. These guys look more like a group of Che Guevara's irregulars than the parade ground toy soldiers I'm used to.

Their Land Rover has also seen too much operational service. It's battered and bent from the bricks that have been hurled at it and is also splashed with the same paint. It has a piece of angle iron welded in place vertically at the front, to cut any piano wire that might have been stretched across a road to decapitate anyone standing up in the back of it.

'Welcome to our world,' they might have said.

They tell me they haven't slept for two days, having been called out on both previous nights to deal with civil unrest, and that I shouldn't feel too sorry for my prisoner, as they've been covering for him in his absence. I hand him over to military justice and get a signature for him.

The rest of us are met by a military bus, which has been cunningly disguised. It's been re-sprayed white. No one will ever guess! Packed with chattering squaddies, it wends its way, with an escort vehicle, out of the docks through the Belfast streets. I look out over what might be any city in Great Britain, except that every other street corner here has a sandbag bunker manned by armed soldiers and police. Cars are being pulled over at random and searched. People are being frisked as they enter shopping areas. Unionist flags and bunting flap in the breeze across many of the side streets. Graffiti gives an insight into what the streets think is important. The odd burnt-out shop and car carcass adds to the prevailing warlike theme. You might be forgiven for thinking this was one day after a tough night before, but it was a way of life here – just one day in four years for a city in torment. It's an eye opener.

The bus pulls up at a junction, as a convoy of armoured vehicles with blue lights sweep by, sirens wailing. From the cat's face transfers on the vehicle doors, I know it's one of our teams on a call from Albert Street Mill.

The countryside approaches and, as the bus leaves the city, I have time to ponder. What do I know about my enemy? Well, I know that whilst Ulster is only the size of Yorkshire, PIRA operates freely across it and has effectively tied up thousands of security forces for many years. I know that this is PIRA's home ground. They know the hills, valleys and city alleys like the backs of their hands. Living here means they aren't out of place when they carry out a reconnaissance. They can't be distinguished from the populace since they don't report for duty in uniform. That very ordinary looking bloke – the farm labourer who holds the gate open as you drive through – might well be the assassin who shot that police officer in the back of the head last week. Or perhaps he's an interrogator called in to torture his own people accused of touting. The Security Forces probably have intelligence on him already, but he has a real advantage – our liberalised legal system. Until any one of them actually commits a crime and there is evidence of it, they can't be arrested. By then of course more people have died. When the perpetrators are brought to trial, the forensic evidence by which they are linked to the crime will be explained in court so that they don't make the same mistakes the next time around. Jail, however, is arguably a holiday camp, or at the very least a training camp, and in a few years these criminals will be out to participate in the mayhem once again.

For simpletons like me, this is democracy fighting with 'our hands tied behind the back'. It's hard for anyone to dispute it even if they prefer it as it is. Going forward, though, can covert, irregular organisations bent on destruction be dealt with quickly using peacetime, democratic means? Watch this space!

The bus deposits us at the British Army HQ at Lisburn and, after attending to some administrative matters, I'm picked up by a car and transported to Lisanelly Barracks at Omagh. On the way, we stop off at the old knicker factory in Lurgan, which is now 3 Brigade Headquarters, and I meet our guys at the section there.

On joining the team in Omagh I discover that we are located with and supporting the resident battalion, the 1st Royal Tank Regiment. The 'tankies' are effectively performing an infantry role from their peacetime location.

Our tactical area of responsibility encompasses much of Tyrone and Fermanagh, which is a large area with a porous international border. The team is headed up by Staff Sergeant Lew Bean. Lew is known by the units he supports as the ATO, since, in Northern Ireland, all operators are collectively called Ammunition Technical Officers, or ATOs for short. ATOs could be any rank from sergeant through to captain.

The previous August, the operator based at Omagh, Ron Beckett, had been killed attempting to deal with a device in the post office at Pettigo: a little village on our western border. It is highly likely that he was killed by a secondary device designed to get him. No one could afford to relax for a second.

Green vehicle movements are allowed throughout the counties of Tyrone and Fermanagh, unlike South Armagh, and we traverse them daily in support of Security Force (SF) operations. I'm not too happy, however, at being issued with a mere 9mm pistol since I know that even in the hands of an expert they are effective only up to about 30 metres – useless frankly. I, therefore, carry one of the team's 12-bore semi-automatic shotguns loaded with a mixture of shot. It's not as effective as a high velocity rifle, but the rifled solid shot gives me some degree of confidence. I guess it's fortunate that I never had to use it against a person or I would have been in trouble, since I'm sure it wasn't approved for use in that way and I would almost certainly have infringed the rights of anyone trying to kill me.

The only high-velocity shots I hear fired in anger during that tour are from me – and then it was only at a car. On this occasion, we are called to clear a vehicle, which has been abandoned on the border. When we arrive, the air is thick with mosquitoes. Some of the troops who have been on the ground for some time can hardly see; their faces are so swollen. Lew wants the car cleared quickly. I say I can help to do this if I can be provided with a rifle, which I duly am. In those days, I was still a bit of a marksman. I put two shots into the fuel tank and then reload the rifle with a tracer round, which I put into the growing pool of leaking fuel. The car burns out and so we can be sure there was nothing sinister contained inside it. We are out of there in double-quick-time and so are the ground troops. Any innovation that helps get the thing completed from a distance is what's called for and you make the best use of anything you can get your hands on. That's a fairly well-established philosophy.

I hope Lew will not mind me saying that he is a prime example of someone who, despite neutralising a number of large devices and being a credit to the corps, didn't receive recognition for it. This may not have bothered him too much, but later on it made me think.

We get around the estate in a Safari five-door Land Rover, which has a horse box attached that is designed to take our Remote Control Vehicle Wheelbarrow. If we have to turn the Land Rover around quickly in a narrow lane, it is a logistical, time-consuming nightmare. This vehicle configuration would soon be superseded by lightly armoured Ford Transits. In fact, all the equipment and technology available to us was changing apace throughout this period. New versions of Wheelbarrow would come on stream every few months, as would new explosive tools and, especially welcome, were improvements in the equipment for tackling radio controlled devices. Whilst there was no shortage of investment by the MoD and we considered the equipment as the front end of technology, this period precedes the digital age. Mechanical switches would fail, CCTV pictures were mono and subject to all the foibles that beset televisions at that time. The remote equipment would often break down, couldn't operate on soft ground and, by today's standards, was extremely clumsy. Nonetheless, we all had great faith in it and it is to the credit of all those who designed, built and modified the stuff that many lives – especially ATOs – were saved.

Getting around the area by vehicle was time-consuming so occasionally we resorted to helicopters. I have to say that, from the air, the undulating countryside of both these rural counties was a picture book of little villages, green fields and silver lakes. To provide a flavour of the tour, I've summarised it with photos taken at some of the incidents we covered.

Main street Castelderg. As
we arrived on the scene a
small device exploded in the
car. The ATO is taking a
quick look.

In case there is a secondary
device the ATO has set the
car on fire since a burnt
out car is a car cleared. We
await events as I reel in the
electrical firing cable.

Above: Two SF landrovers were ambushed making their way back from supporting us in an investigation of a bus explosion in Lisnaskea. A Command Wire device detonated under the road caused the second landrover to somersault up the road. The only reason our team didn't use this road is that we attended the bus incident by helicopter.

The escort in the front passenger seat wasn't thrown clear and he was crushed by the vehicle. This was the first body I had ever seen and I was somewhat transfixed by the tragedy. The ATO had to snap me out of my contemplation. I was always shocked by similar sights because they brought home just how mortal we all are and how we are potentially just one journey from disaster.

The upper floor of the Deanery at Clogher was used as an operational headquarters for a UDR unit. One evening it came under attack from two groups of gunmen. Mortars and two RPG 7 rockets were also used in the attack. The skeleton staff at the HQ were almost overwhelmed but the day was saved by the co incidental arrival of two Scout cars from the Royal Tank Regiment. During the attack Woman Private Eva Martin *(above right)* was struck in the head as she passed by a staircase window and killed. She was the first woman soldier to die in the Campaign.

PIRA mortar bombs abandoned during the attack. The ATO has asked me to remove their propelling charges prior to destroying them in a controlled explosion.

An explosion was reported at this barn We found blood and a part collapsed roof so an `own goal' was suspected. However we also detected a radio control signal.

After jamming any radio control firing signal the ATO went forward and discovered a milk churn under the collapsed roof.

He then discovered another milk churn and subsequently two more. These were all linked by detonating cord.

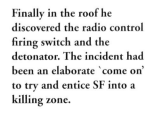

Finally in the roof he discovered the radio control firing switch and the detonator. The incident had been an elaborate `come on' to try and entice SF into a killing zone.

After intercepting two armed men in a car SF decided to investigate this remote farm.

SF found this large car bomb in situ which was apparently on its way to Enniskillen.

In fact the whole place was a Quartermasters store of arms and bomb making equipment.

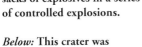

Above: We destroyed five sacks of explosives in a series of controlled explosions.

Below: This crater was produced by just one sack of the Home Made Explosives.

Under this small bridge SF discovered a large device in milk churns which would have been detonated by Command Wire.

One milk churn has been extracted, more to follow.

Destroying the device is a series of controlled explosions.

The out station at Rosslea was attacked one night by Proxy.
The driver who'd been hijacked and had a bomb loaded onto
his van left it outside the security wall but didn't tell anyone.
Fortunately despite the extensive damage there were no
casualties. Interestingly there was absolutely nothing left that
was discernible of the van.

'Keeping my eye in.' Trying
out the Trilux 'zoot' sight on
ranges north of Omagh

We didn't have far to travel to this one - about 200 metres from
Lisanelly camp. We worked on the van bomb for about 30
minutes from the other side of the building, but our equipment
became tangled at the sharp end in our firing cables. Eventually
we fired the `flying plate ' Beguine even though it had spun
around and was facing the wrong way (see chapter from the
Passive to the Offensive). The vehicle caught fire but 15 minutes
later the device functioned. You end up struggling with your
mate to get in or under the team vehicle because you know that
everything that went up is going to come down.

Flying Plate Beguine on its stand (covered for security reasons) at the ATO's office, Omagh. Cables became entangled when we used it for real at the Crown Buildings incident.

The Crown building was wrecked. 5,000 chickens held in an adjacent farm were decimated and our Remote Control Equipment Wheelbarrow was written off.

Towards the end of my four-month tour at the Omagh Section, I was transferred to the Headquarters at Lisburn, primarily to assist the Warrant Officer ATO who was seconded to the Forensic Science Laboratory near Belfast. An incident occurred at Lisburn, which is worth mentioning because I think it helps to illustrate that operators, despite the Hollywood hype, are really nothing more or less than a cross-section of the populace with all the idiosyncrasies and personality weaknesses that people get by with. I call this incident the 'Isandlwana moment' and it went like this:

'Foxtrot' is the reserve team based at Lisburn and it hasn't been deployed for quite some time. The team's vehicle has, therefore, been de-kitted of all its equipment. Our HQ was closed at night and in order that the duty operator can access the equipment during silent hours it is kept in the cellar at the HQ Lisburn guardroom. On this occasion, it is about midday and a 'disruption day' is on the go in Belfast. A number of car bombs are being dealt with and all the Belfast teams have been committed. The Foxtrot team, in the military vernacular, is to be 'stood to' so that it can respond immediately to an operational tasking order when it comes. I am told to get myself over to the guardroom, asap, to help a certain ATO captain get Foxtrot up and running. I approach the guardroom at the gallop and, as I do, the wind in my ears doesn't prevent me from hearing a strange sound emanating from the guardroom: a sort of strangled cry like someone in pain, or perhaps even a wounded animal.

'What the hell is that?' I wonder, as you do.

Bursting into the guardroom, I scan the room and it is easy to see from the worried faces of the soldiers standing around that all is not well. And, sure enough, there comes another strangled cry, followed by some crashing and thumping from the cellar.

'Where's the ATO?' I ask, somewhat unnecessarily, for already a possible scenario is beginning to dawn on me.

Someone points to the stairs and apprehensively I descend. I am greeted, as they say, by an amazing sight. The ATO, red in face and breathing heavily, has completely lost it. The reason is sitting defiantly between us on the floor of the cellar. The Quartermaster, for accounting and security purposes, has had the Foxtrot team equipment neatly packed into a wooden crate and this has been securely bound with metal banding tape. If cutting equipment had originally been left there, there was certainly no evidence of it now and no way of accessing the team equipment.

The ATO's despair, frustration and anger at the situation had got the better of him and he was now looking for someone to kill. At that moment he was taking it out on the crate.

As I watch from the safety of the staircase, the officer gives a further strangled cry and, cursing and swearing, he launches himself once more at the crate, booting it with both feet in turn, but, alas, in vain. It was, with hindsight, pure comedy of the *Fawlty Towers* ilk. Gasping to catch his breath for a moment, he pauses and I see my opportunity. I leap across the room to place myself between him and the abused box. I ask him to calm down. The reputation of the cool, calm and collected ATO is now in tatters, at least at the Lisburn HQ guardroom. He responds surprisingly well to the suggestion and so I don't have to hit him.

After that, someone shoots off to the stores to get some cutting equipment and eventually, with the Improvised Explosive Device Disposal (IEDD) kit loaded onto his vehicle, we send him off to the war. I'll give him his due, he did thank me afterwards for my help in getting him through what he thought was a short period of stress. He was, however, highly strung at the best of times and had a reputation for smashing telephone receivers. But this, shall we say, personality quirk, hadn't prevented him from becoming an operator. The psychometric testing we all had to undergo wasn't a very useful tool if it was supposed to filter out at source the temperamental. In fact, I'm sceptical as to whether it really filtered out anyone who was really unsuitable, since a veritable cross-section of characters always remained within the profession. There is no stereotype that you can call on to represent a bomb disposal operator, even if people like to think there is.

I have likened the Lisburn guardroom incident to the disaster at Isandlwana in South Africa in 1879. Here it was with a Zulu army bearing down on them that the British troops found out, too late, that, for accounting and security purposes, the Quartermaster had centralised the rifle ammunition and it was held in inaccessible packaging. You'll know this if you've seen the film *Zulu Dawn*. On that earlier occasion, the troops were going to be put to the assegai, so I have every sympathy with them if they had wanted to strangle the Quartermaster.

The Kineton Sergeants' Mess

At the end of my tour I return to Kineton and back to the 'bread and butter' work of the Ammunition Technician. Towards the end of 1974 I'm promoted to Local Acting (and unpaid!) Sergeant, since the unit is short of senior ranks, and move into the Sergeants' Mess. This is perhaps the biggest step for a soldier, for the traditions of the Mess give the army a completely different complexion. All these years on, I still remember my initial feelings. Everything changed from what I had experienced before; it is so much more civilised. Dining is waitress service; there is a bar in the building; newspapers are provided; coffee is on tap.

There is also a sink in my room, whereas, for junior ranks, the ablutions are a shared commodity. With these privileges, of course, comes greater responsibility.

My first regimental dinner is another life changing experience. The regimental dinner is a mainstay of the regimental system. They are funded by the soldiers themselves who pay fees into a Mess account. As the most junior member of the Mess, I'm appointed 'Mr Vice'. My task is to toast the Commander in Chief, i.e. Her Majesty the Queen. The RSM briefs me in advance as to my duty.

'When the port decanter is returned to my table, the President of the Mess Committee will bang the gavel three times. He will say, "Mr Vice". You will stand up, lift your port glass and say, "Ladies and Gentlemen – the Queen". There will be no pause before saying "the Queen". Do you have any questions? No? Then do not make any mistakes.'

Any such mistakes, I knew, would incur extra duties.

We gather in the ante room at 7.30 p.m. The sherry is served to the hundred or so Mess members. All are dressed in their Royal Army Ordnance Corps red and navy blue Mess dress finery. Many uniforms are adorned with shiny miniature medals. The gong sounds at 8 p.m. and everyone walks through into the large dining room. In this large candlelit room, the tables are laid to perfection with the cutlery, glasses, silverware and trophies. Again, it's easy to take it for granted now, but coming from a working class background, seeing all this for the first time, was breathtaking.

People take their seat according to the seating plan. The Warrant Officer's Class 1 sit at the top table with the guests and the remainder of us sit according to our seniority on either side of the two long legs. As 'Mr Vice' I sit on the very end of the longest leg – barely in the room!

Fortunately, I did not cock up my duty, despite traditional attempts by 'friends' to sabotage my efforts. All in all, it's a very relaxed evening and extremely enjoyable.

Prior to this event I have to admit that I had been reflecting on my options and even toying with the idea of leaving the army. From here on in, all such negative thoughts dissipate and I commit myself to a full career.

My role at Kineton is much more supervisory now and I'm allocated a series of Ammunition Process Buildings to oversee. In these earth-banked, concrete buildings, like at Bracht in Germany, the full range of ammunition natures would be unpacked and worked on by Ammo Techs, supported by Supply Specialists (male and female) and civilian labourers. I would visit regularly, checking on safety, working practices, ensuring the proper equipment was being used, checking on cleanliness and answering questions. I got well into it.

It's probably worth mentioning that this is the year that my first brush with religion occurred. Through my cousin, Alan, I become interested in a South

London-based religious sect called the Divine Light Mission. At the time it is rapidly expanding across the country, drawing some pretty adverse press, since it is headed up by a fifteen–year-old Indian lad call Guru Maharaji (or, to give him his full title, Balyogeshwarparamhans satgurudev shri sans ji maharesh – a bit of a mouthful, eh! It's amazing I can still remember it compared to all the important things I've forgotten!)

This organisation, which obviously arose out of the Indian sub-continent, provides a somewhat scientific view of god and the universe, which is quite in keeping with the times (Lyalls Watson's *Supernature* and all that). The teaching definitely strikes a chord. Their pacifist thinking, however, doesn't entirely sit well with my chosen career and after a few brushes with my hierarchy, together with an early realisation that the people who have the most say in these organisations aren't as divine as they think they are, I leave.

The organisation is still around today, albeit with a different title, but it is much lower key. It has also adopted a different set of priorities than that of converting the world.

The remainder of 1974 is notable mainly for the fact that my future wife, Jen, a member of the Women's Royal Army Corps, and I first get together and that Vern Rose and John Maddocks don't return from the Long Walk. The following year we are married.

Jen and I were married on a sunny but blustery day in Halifax 1975. A long time together, five great children, but by 2000 we weren't getting on.

2ND TOUR NI — 1975–76

In July, newly promoted to substantive (and paid!) sergeant and married only a fortnight, I'm posted out of Kineton, back to the conflict in Ireland. This time it's as a member of the permanent staff of 321 Explosive Ordnance Disposal (EOD) Company at the British Army Headquarters in Lisburn. The unit had been formed specifically to carry out and coordinate Bomb Disposal Operations in Ulster. Prior to the Northern Ireland conflict, no such unit existed.

For me it's a twelve-month stint as an operator, but it is also my job to handle the unit's reports and to collate statistical data.

Being an accompanied posting, Jen and I are provided with a married quarter at Headquarters Northern Ireland. It is quite civilised, but at times it is quite surreal. People could get energised about stock checks and audits, etc. So, on the one hand, it felt like a peacetime posting and, when normality reigned, it seemed, well, normal. On the other hand, I could spend a day sweating it out down town, which on any given day might have more in common with Beirut in the bad old days than Great Britain. When I return to the Mess, however, the topic would still be about stock checks and bloody audits.

Within a week of taking up the post the team from Bessbrook drop in to pick up some equipment. We briefly touch on old times, since WO2 Gus Garside, the operator, had been one of my instructors at the apprentice college and his No. 2, Corporal Cal Brown, is a friend and colleague from CAD Kineton, the unit I had just left. I remember that moment well all these years on; their faces are fixed in my mind. Within a week, however, the team has been wiped out. They are both killed with two other soldiers as they deploy from a helicopter at a crossroads near Forkhill in an operation to deal with some suspicious objects that are preventing the crossroads from being used as a vehicle check point. A device comprising 50–100lb of home-made explosives (HME) dug into the roadside is detonated as they negotiate a stile at the edge of a field. The Command Wire-type device was initiated by a local unemployed coach builder who, on seeing the opportunity, had scrambled to a vantage point across the other side of the field. As a result of this tragedy, our Render Safe Procedures (RSPs) in the rural areas are amended. The bomber is arrested that same afternoon by a soldier who had seen him in the lane immediately before the explosion.

The team's belongings are repatriated via the HQ at Lisburn. Their damaged weapons and burnt flack jackets are a sad and sorry sight.

The two headquarters teams have an operational area of responsibility, which covers Counties Antrim and some of County Down, and also provides a backup to the Belfast Section. As a member of the HQ back office staff, however, an operator isn't immune to the omnipresent dangers, and on one particular February morning in 1976, my day starts calmly enough, but this changes when I am unexpectedly caught up in a big, fast-moving incident. By the end of the day it has almost ended in disaster.

Called in to support the Belfast Section, my team and I are tasked to provide cover for the city centre. Accordingly, we are deployed to the Grand Central Hotel on Royal Avenue – or GCH, as it was called – to await events. This old Victorian hotel was at the end of its natural life and was being used as a barracks for a few hundred soldiers. It was often a target for car bombs, but not so often that I might have anticipated it happening today. So, sure enough, PIRA attack it via the adjacent GPO sorting office building. I would find out later that the sorting office was separated from the GCH by only a narrow street that ran parallel to Royal Avenue. This narrow street was within the GCH security complex and the military used it as a vehicle park.

The first I know that we are under attack is when the bomb alarm goes off with a deafening wail and the well-practised evacuation drill kicks in for real. The place immediately bursts into life with soldiers pouring out of every room and spilling down the main staircase into Royal Avenue. If I was to know what was going on I would have to get to the ops room on an upper floor, but this isn't easy. My work is cut out just trying to get up the stairs, since there is a veritable wall of soldiers travelling equally forcibly in the opposite direction. Eventually, arriving at the ops room, I find the staff there are more concerned with evacuating the room than briefing me. All I get from a captain, as he pushed past me with a pile of files in his arms, is, 'There's a bomb in the GPO sorting office.'

Before I can say, 'Where the hell is the sorting office?' he is gone! I don't remember a scenario anything like this on the Pre-ops course exercises. There you'd ask a pertinent question and, by jingo, you received a pertinent answer – which is a good basis for decision making.

To be on scene at this very early juncture is unusual for an operator and I am now caught up in the confusion and chaos that accompanies the evacuation of the buildings. With no tangible information to go on, my mind is racing, trying to work out what to do next. I also soon realise that accessing the team equipment is going to be problematic once I discover that our vehicle is inconveniently parked up against the sorting office building wall. As I tentatively peer around the street corner, contemplating whether we should risk a sortie into the danger area to recover it, a smallish device explodes in the sorting office with a loud bang that echoes up and down the narrow street, blowing out some windows on the first floor. I then see that the building hadn't been fully evacuated of civilians. Forward of the security cordon, now without a radio, I am on the spot. Metaphorically speaking, I take off my ATO hat and behave as I think any member of the Security Forces would: I carry out a quick foray into the building to make sure no one else remained, calling out as I go. There isn't and, for my trouble, as I am leaving a mezzanine floor, a second small device detonates above a doorway just a second or two after I have walked through it. Either I stumble or the blast blows me down the staircase. I land upside-down in a heap at the bottom of the stairwell, covered in plaster. I am unharmed, but I have the strange sensation that the hairs on the back of my neck are quite erect. I pick myself up and stumble to the building entrance. You can imagine my surprise, however, when I discover that I have been locked in behind fifteen-foot metal gates. The boilerman (whose very presence had caused me to enter the building) had left the scene, but only after securing the gates behind him. I only manage to escape the building after my No. 2, Lance Corporal Coates, discovering my predicament, goes off and drags the boilerman back to the gate.

Someone prematurely shouted, 'The ATO's copped it!' and before I can even catch my breath, the security cordon around GCH collapses. To my dismay, I am faced with a whole bevy of soldiers heading towards me down the narrow street. With two small devices having functioned and the high likelihood that a much bigger one was not far behind them, a lot of people are about to be killed. I am suddenly gripped by fear. In my urgency to get everyone out of the danger area I'm afraid I am none too polite in requesting the soldiers leave the scene. Let me state now, a little late, my apologies to the Commanding Officer of the Regiment whom I didn't recognise till afterwards and who got the worst of my tongue!

A few minutes later, we are all safe at the front of GCH in Royal Avenue and the cordon is re-established. Breathing heavily and with my hands shaking like leaves in a storm, I realise, all of a sudden, that I am surrounded by people. Royal Avenue is teeming with both civilians and soldiers. People are asking me lots of questions and I can't give many answers. I'm a bit shocked I guess. I'm trying to pull myself together when, all of a sudden, a substantial 'baboom' thunders out from the other side of the GCH building. It is a massive blast that sounds something like the van bomb at the Crown Buildings, Omagh, two years ago. The effect was to blow away all the hubbub around me and, for a split second, there is silence. The silence is followed almost immediately by the familiar tinkling sound of glass falling like heavy rain into the streets behind me.

I would discover later that I had unknowingly walked past the van bomb when I was checking out the place. Had there been any delay in clearing the area, we would have lost a lot of soldiers.

Above: Aftermath. The narrow street which separated the Grand Central Hotel on the left from the GPO Sorting Office on the right. Military vehicles damaged by the blast remain in situ.

Below: PW in discussion with the Royal Engineer Searchers post final clearance. On the left is Scouse Manley an RE member of 67B Apprentice Group. It's a small world!

Left: The spot, up against the wall where our team vehicle (Foxtrot) had been parked. Inside the building the large diesel tank that the fire brigade had been so worried about can just be seen.

Below: As I walked around this scene of devastation the next day I contemplated just how tenuous life can be as an ATO and it's not only your life that's on the line, your entire career can be up there too for mistakes are not easily forgiven.

The damage was quite extensive to all rooms on that side of the GCH building, not to mention the sorting office. A breeze block guardroom built on to the GCH as a blister was completely wrecked. Some military Land Rovers were written off and security sensitive papers, which had been sucked out of various shattered windows, were now blowing around the street, much to the annoyance of their owners, running around trying to collect them all up. My armoured vehicle was barely driveable since it had sustained a damaged wheel and was stripped of its blue light and aerials and covered in rubble.

Control was tightened up and no one was to be allowed into the danger area. I was approached then by the Fire Brigade who wanted to enter the area to extinguish a fire that was threatening a 5,000-gallon tank of diesel used for refuelling GPO vehicles. They insisted and so I took the opportunity, with my No. 2, to go forward with them and reconnoitre the damage. We pulled all the rubble off our vehicle and then Lance Corporal Coates recovered it. I watched as it limped away into safety with its seriously wobbly wheel. We all withdrew behind the cordon then and thirty minutes later a further, small device detonated in the same building. With daylight fading fast the sorting office was secured overnight and no one was allowed in.

Overall, a disaster had been averted simply by good luck more than anyone's good judgement.

The building was searched the next day and found to be clear of any further devices. Although I had to destroy a suspicious duffle bag in a controlled explosion, which turned out to be someone's abandoned lunch.

This incident demonstrates how dangers unexpectedly and quickly strike from nowhere when you live and work within this field. As much as you might try to apply the training principles, fast-moving events can get the better of you. When this happens, and you have done something wrong, then you're in trouble. I'm pretty certain that if I or anyone else had been killed or injured in the incident then I, as the operator at the scene, would probably have received a good deal of flack over it. The chaos and confusion that reigned at the time would have been history by the time my role and immediate actions were analysed in the light of our strict operating procedures. The profession was bound up by this type of thinking at that time and I'll comment further on this matter later in the book. As it happened, the incident was passed off as a fairly routine matter. Lt Colonel Underhill was interviewed that evening in the street by Trevor McDonald for the BBC News to explain to the Ulster people why their mail was going to be delivered a little later than usual.

In the immediate aftermath of the vehicle bomb explosion, a policeman brought a postman over to me and I was able to ask him a few questions. It was he who had driven the large vehicle bomb into the sorting office. At the time, I thought he'd been coerced into it, but later he would admit to some complicity. I guess he could have said he'd acted under duress, since proxy type incidents were very common at this time.

Later that year I was sitting in the Crumlin Road Crown Court when the sentence was passed. Well, to be honest, I felt only sadness for him and his family. Living in Andersons Town, a mainly Republican area, he had been made an offer to drive the bomb that he couldn't refuse and in the end he was probably the only real victim of the incident. He was the same age as me. Despite protestations that he had never been a member of PIRA and the efforts of his brief to mitigate his role in the attack, he was sent down for fifteen years.

During this tour I have my fair share of incendiary devices to deal with. These devices are mainly of Protestant origin; they are often

PROXY BOMBS

PIRA would often hijack a vehicle with two occupants. A bomb would be loaded on board. Holding one of the occupants hostage, the other would be ordered to drive the vehicle and bomb to a target. If the vehicle was stopped on the way to the target the Security Forces had to remember they were dealing with innocent parties. Many attacks were less than successful since the vehicle would often be abandoned by its frightened owner without being placed in the optimum spot. Nonetheless this modus operandi significantly reduced the risk to PIRA members.

crude and targeted against Catholics living in the Larne area. On one occasion, because the room is inaccessible to my remote control equipment, I have to enter it myself. The floor is covered in diesel fuel and, right in the middle of it, two small incendiary devices in cigarette packets have been placed with the intention of igniting the fuel. I'm not sure how much the suit would have protected me if the whole thing had gone up. Having your No. 2 standing by with a fire extinguisher was always a good idea in these circumstances.

On another occasion, two incendiary devices placed on a bus are subsequently confirmed by the Forensic Science Laboratory as having chemical components that did not, in fact, react with each other – and so the devices are effectively inert. This knowledge subsequently leads me to adopt a Render Safe Procedure that with hindsight I wished I'd tackled differently.

One evening, I am tasked to deal with an attack that has occurred on a Catholic school in Larne. Prior to my arrival, someone has gallantly (or foolishly, depending on your point of view) placed the device into a sand-filled bucket, which has been left on top of a desk. The device itself comprises about 5kg of an incendiary mix contained inside a large glass chemical bottle. The switch is of a chemical delay type, like the devices on the bus previously. This chemical initiator is half-stuffed into the neck of the bottle, and the bottle is, unfortunately, well-protected from my disruptive equipment by the sides of the metal bucket. What to do?

I surmise that, because the previous incendiary devices had been inert this might well be the same. I, therefore, decide to risk lifting out the chemical initiator. Briefing my No. 2, Corporal Spencer, I ask him to wait outside the room with a fire extinguisher at the ready. Taking a deep breath, I lean over the desk and take a firm hold of the initiator. It is tight and at first it won't budge. I pull a little harder and then – 'pssst' – it is the telltale sound of acid dropping onto the incendiary mix. The device initiates and I just have time to throw myself backwards across the room. Increasing in intensity, and with a roar, the device goes up like a regular Vesuvius. As the bottle melts before my very eyes, the white hot flames soar up, peeling the paint from the high classroom ceiling. This inferno lasts for about five to ten seconds. Right on cue, Corporal Spencer appears in the doorway with the fire extinguisher in hand and a look on his face as if he was expecting to have to turn it on me. His arrival is about the only thing that went right with the plan, for the CO_2 extinguisher was useless against the oxygenated inferno. Nonetheless, it would prevent the flames from spreading had they not been confined to the sand-filled bucket. As jet-black smoke fills up the room, I am grateful that the thing hasn't exploded. Little collateral damage, but, I have to say, this is not my finest moment.

Throughout my time with the headquarters, the ops phone on my desk would ring and, with just a short explanation of the task, the location and the contact at the scene, the duty team would crash out. Often the calls would occur in the middle of the night and when I was the duty operator the team would collect me from my married quarter. On one occasion, my mother came to stay with us. Woken up by both the blue flashing lights and the animated radio traffic, it was a bit disconcerting for her to see her only son disappear on a mission to God knows where, fearing I was never going to come back. With the benefit of hindsight, I recommend operators don't let their mothers get that close to the action! Again, it was this Lisburn anomaly of being a peacetime unit, but very much part of a war.

Above: This is one of the aerial photographs that was used to plan the operation at Cortreasla Bridge that resulted in the deaths of the ATO, his Number 2, a Company Commander in the Green Howards and an RE Search Adviser. As the soldiers negotiated a stile, a device buried alongside the sign post was detonated by a Command Wire . The guy who murdered them was arrested that afternoon. General Sir Richard Dannatt late Commander in Chief of UK Land Forces was at this incident as a young officer.

Middle: The driver of this Proxy- type device had been ordered to take a bomb into Aldergrove airport. Bravely he drove the vehicle through the airport complex to some waste ground where the device eventually exploded harmlessly.

Left: This is Bow Street in Lisburn where my wife and I would often go shopping. I had just received the tasking message from HQ 39 Brigade when the room shook as the vehicle- borne device detonated.

Above: A weekend of disruption by Protestant militants had all teams in and around Belfast flat out dealing with hundreds of hoax devices. A complete distraction. The picture shows four I was tasked to. Hoax devices could be quite sophisticated. The cylinder on the left even has a mercury tilt switch wired in. All the time I was dealing with these devices the radio traffic was red hot with the SF on the ground at Randlestown pleading for ATO assistance for a car bomb. Eventually the car bomb went off before anyone was tasked to it.

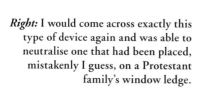

WELDED CAST
PIPE BOMBS

Right: I would come across exactly this type of device again and was able to neutralise one that had been placed, mistakenly I guess, on a Protestant family's window ledge.

Left: This is a Protestant UVF terrorist cache of bomb-making materials. I spent a lot of time chasing them around Antrim dealing with their devices – at least 5 were probably down to them. I got the impression over time that the Protestant terrorist organisations were even more ruthless in their targetting than PIRA.

Below: I gave evidence at the court case that sent down the UVF boys whose explosive cache it was and who wore these masks. At the trial the defence lawyer fiercely grilled a police office for ages who had been shot by one of them, such that I offered my sympathy to him when we met up later. He told me that at one point he had begun to wonder whether he had in fact been shot at all.

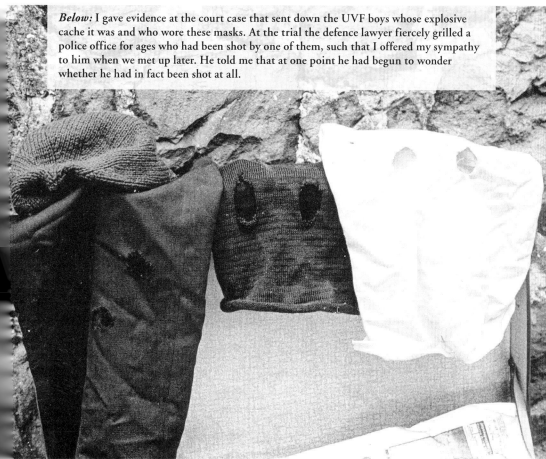

Within a week of completing my tour I was called to Antrim to deal with a truck load of mortars pointing into the Royal Navy Armaments Depot and adjacent army camp. The army had had the foresight to block the flight path of the mortars with the shovel of an armoured digger.

After firing the two rounds of 84mm Carl Gustav at the truck to disrupt the electrical firing leads I blew the tyres on one side of the truck with a series of small explosive charges.

The Sapper driver of the armoured Digger gallantly agreed to tip the truck over.

We recovered 18 home made mortar bombs and their tubes. Note the dent in one tube caused by the impact of a Carl Gustav projectile. The attack failed primarily because the mortar switching arrangement had self destructed before it could fire the actual mortars. Within a short time this type of mortar bomb would be obsolete and PIRA would replace it with a bomb that had 30 times the payload and was a lot less complicated. For my contribution the RNAD presented me with a brass replica of a Londonderry cannon called Old Meg. I still have it.

Left: Workmen reported an explosion in close proximity to their hut at a building site in Lisburn. At first there was no obvious evidence of this and I have Wheelbarrow carrying out a recce.

Middle: At some point you have to make an approach. Here I am searching around and under the hut, and there it was, jammed in between the hut and the adjacent wall. Not easy to get at.

Below: The device in a Tupperware container had partially exploded in that the detonator had functioned but this had not propogated to the main charge. The type of explosives would suggest that the device was of a Protestant terrorist origin.

Left: Strips of Detonating Cord at the ready I'm going to explosively open the doors of this suspect car which has been abandoned outside Aldergrove Airport 1976.

Middle: Lisburn Section 'Foxtrot' team vehicle, 1 ton armoured Humber(a 'Pig'). It got a pounding at the GPO Sorting Office in Belfast Feb 1976.

Below: 1975. Headquarters staff of 321 EOD Company outside the Portakabin at Lisburn. Lt Col Underhill the Chief ATO is reflecting the sunlight and to his right is the Senior ATO at the time, Major Archer. Next to him is the Senior Ammo Tech, WO1 Fred Moughton. I'm standing with my friend Api Nanova – a Fijian.

One of the buggerance factors of serving in NI as an operator was the subsequent court cases we were called to attend as expert witnesses. These attendances were highly onerous for some people who were called back from all parts of the world, time and time again. People were brought back from Hong Kong, for example, only to have the case deferred for weeks or cancelled. Often the date for a hearing would be moved even as the ATO was in transit to it. Sometimes, if your case was deferred or cancelled, the first you'd hear of it was in the Crumlin Road Court House café after standing around for two days waiting to be called. This café was a melting pot of defendants, their families and also their accusers. It was bizarre. For a start no one in authority seemed to have any concerns over the costs of this little lot or the time that was being wasted. If behind the scenes it was all spiffingly efficient, well, it certainly didn't feel like that to us. On one particular occasion, though, I did feel that my attendance at court had been especially useful.

In the dock was a Protestant terrorist gang who had caused mayhem in the Larne area over a period of years. I think we'd met before in the abstract sense. These boys were trying to muddy the waters at their trial by claiming the SAS (Special Air Service) had been involved in the murder of a leading Catholic, which they were being accused of. They said the Special Air Service had put them up to it. Evidence for the defence involved a British army ammunition container that the gang insisted had been given to them by the SAS.

Almost as a throwaway comment, the prosecution barrister asked me if I knew anything about ammunition boxes, to which I replied, 'I do.' Taking me into a room, he showed me the box in question. It was grey in colour and had 'SAS' stencilled on it in white paint. He asked me if Special Air Service ammunition containers would normally have the regiment's name written on them. Later that day, I was called to the witness box to give evidence in the same case in respect of a blast bomb I had neutralised. I was asked to explain how I had gone about it and the damage it would have done had it functioned. After I had given my evidence, the barrister suggested to the judge that I may be able to clarify matters in respect of the ammunition box and this was duly passed across for me to interpret the markings on it. It gave me great pleasure to be able to say that the box was a standard military package with standard markings. The grey paint signified that the box would have contained chemical ammunition of the lachrymatory type, i.e. CS gas. Because the ammunition in an accident would produce irritant smoke, when transported by sea it must always be stored on deck. SAS, therefore, signified that the ammunition container required Special Ammunition Stowage. The waters were less muddy at the trial after that.

I end this tour having attended a particularly nasty incident which, ruthless as they are, seems somewhat out of keeping with PIRA's normal modus operandi.

At about 10 p.m. on 25th May at Walker's Bar in Templepatrick, a predominately Protestant pub, a car roars up and two masked men step out, one with an ArmaLite Rifle. They are approached by an elderly chap employed by the pub to watch out for anything suspicious: a bomb watcher. He is immediately shot down. A seventeen-year-old car park attendant is also gunned down and when his sister remonstrated with the gunmen she is also shot. As people scramble in panic to escape by the back door, one gunman fires into the bar injuring another person and the other, shouting, 'To hell with the lot of you,' lobs something into the bar area.

By the time I arrive, about thirty minutes later, the suspect device hasn't functioned. Whilst the injured have been taken to hospital, the two male victims out front remain where they have fallen.

My first question to those in charge is, how badly injured are they? This is met with shaking heads. No one has checked them out, fearing the device will function. Whilst it might be an outside chance, one or both could still be alive. A doctor is already present and, with some persuasion, I have to say, he eventually agrees to accompany me and check out the victims. I don't ask for permission from my hierarchy to enter the danger area, I just get on with it.

The two victims lay head to head, blocking the pub entrance. The doctor takes about three seconds to declare them both dead and then scarpers, leaving me to step over them and look into the pub from the doorway. The floor is covered in overturned tables and chairs and broken glasses. I quickly scan the room, not wanting to hang around too long for obvious reasons when, in the centre of the room, I see a cast iron cylindrical tube, which I immediately identified as a PIRA Mk 11 hand grenade. This significantly reduces the risks and, walking over to it, I find that the pin is still in place. I am, therefore, able to recover it intact. The pin is well splayed and, because of this, I suspect the gunman has not been able to extract it and, in exasperation, simply lobbed the grenade into the room. Either that, or he did not entirely share the ruthlessness of his colleague.

Stepping back out of the pub, I look down at the bodies, both face-down, head to head in a pool of dark blood. They seem larger than life with that eerie stillness and relaxed demeanour that no actor can replicate. The sister is pronounced dead on arrival at the hospital.

As I say, it was a thoroughly nasty, despicable sectarian incident but, ruthless as they are, killing unarmed civilians in this indiscriminate manner wasn't how PIRA normally went about their business in Ulster.

I was with the Headquarters one year and in that time I was tasked to a total of seventy-plus incidents. Many involved explosives, of which fourteen were categorised as live devices: mainly blast bombs and incendiaries, together with the incident that found its way onto the front pages of, at least, the *Daily Mirror* which involved the truck full of mortars. My twelve months with the Headquarters was interesting, exciting and often eventful. Notwithstanding the misery the people of Northern Ireland were being put through, I have to say I thoroughly enjoyed my time there.

AMMUNITION INSPECTORATE — 1975–76

We leave Lisburn in May 1976 after I receive a posting to the Ammunition Inspectorate at Colchester. The unit's official title is No. 1 Ammunition Inspection and Disposal Unit, which is a bit of a mouthful and doesn't reflect a recognisable regimental structure. In due course it will be renamed 11 EOD Regiment.

Whilst the Headquarters is based in Hounslow, the unit is effectively deployed in sections across the whole of the UK. From Colchester, we cover the eastern counties of Lincolnshire, Norfolk, Suffolk and parts of Essex.

Our role is primarily to maintain the ammunition stocks held in unit hands (i.e. training stock) and to provide those units with specialist advice. We are also responsible for dealing with terrorist devices outside of London, training police units and providing specialist representation if ammunition is to be loaded onto ships. We also investigate and report on military accidents that have involved ammunition. Finally, we deal with UXBs (unexploded ammunition, which is often found by the public from time to time). During the Second World War, all the eastern counties provided military training facilities and ranges, and the beaches and cliffs were also mined. Now that it's all given back to be farmland, a great deal of UXB-type clag gets churned up by ploughs each year and, if not by the ploughs, there are the metal detector enthusiasts.

Jen and I have an army hiring: a three bedroom semi in St John's Road, which is very nice. Each day I report in to the office where WO1 John Morling hands me a clutch of tasking sheets of UXB-type incidents that have been reported to the Joint EOD Reporting Centre. The incidents have been categorised in terms of priority and I work out an order of travel from the large map of East Anglia on the wall. Collecting a bright red demolition box packed full of explosives from our armoury and a Land Rover, similarly coloured with its bright red wings, I'm off. Sometimes, I have a driver, otherwise, I drive myself. Some days, I drive 3 to 400 miles back and forth across the counties, dealing not only with the original tasks, but also receiving new ones as the day wears on.

I spend a lot of time in police stations, since they are the main contacts on the ground. It's a varied job. There might be a rusty mortar bomb in a field with its fuze rusted solid, or a German 1 kg thermite incendiary bomb, which are frequently found in this area. Occasionally, phosphorous floats used by ships are washed up on the shore. A mound of earth might reveal a thousand spent smoke bombs.

Not what you'd expect to see in Suffolk; a German anti Tank mine. Note the closeness of the plough furrow and also the white 'gunge' around its base which is exuded TNT.

1976. The No 5 Anti Tank Mine. One of a number I dealt with that year on the North Norfolk beaches.

On one occasion, a farmer ploughed up a bank of earth out of which tumbled a large anti-tank mine in excellent condition. It had all the markings of a German Tellar mine. I can only assume that it must have been captured stocks that we had re-laid at some time. I destroy all such items in controlled explosions with small amounts of plastic explosives. It's the quickest and simplest way of dealing with them – and least risky.

The crumbling cliffs of Norfolk held a secret for many years after the war, although the locals were probably well aware of it. The tops were laid with anti-tank mines. I'm not sure how the enemy would get a tank up there, but, anyway, at the end of the war the minefield maps that recorded the positions of these mines were lost. Ongoing erosion meant that live mines would regularly fall out of the cliffs onto the beach. Despite a number of attempts to clear the cliffs and beaches by the authorities, this continued for years. I must have dealt with at least four mines during 1976 alone.

On one visit to north Norfolk I am guided to a cylindrical metal object lying on the beach. It is about 18 inches across and 8 inches or so deep with a large flat metal

Left: Still don't know what it was but it left one helluva hole!

plate welded to one side. Despite it having been reported as a mine I have my doubts. It doesn't look anything like one for a start. There is no pressure plate, for example. Much flotsam gets washed up on those beaches so, frankly, it could be anything. This is going to be waste of time, I think. However, rather than take it away, I decide to be on the safe side and blow it up (at the very least open it up with explosives). It is battered and rusty, so I don't consider it sensitive. I carry it to the cliff face where I had previously dug a small pit. I mould an 8 ounce plastic explosive charge to the item, run out a short firing cable, connect a detonator and give the necessary warnings to the police who had kindly secured the area.

It was just as well that I had taken all appropriate precautions. Far from being empty it must have contained about 20 lbs of TNT. What a thump! It produces a massive crater and brings half the bloody cliff down.

I was never able to properly identify the item, but it taught me that you can't be sure of anything metal you might find rattling around the beaches in East Anglia. The combatants in the Second World War have a lot to answer for.

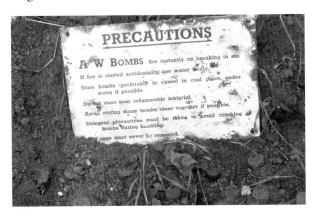

The Albright & Wilson metal sign. All that was left of the SIP Grenade container after 40 years buried at the bottom of a Lowestoft garden. Note the rusty crown cork bottle tops just visible.

On another occasion, I am called to a house near Yarmouth after a member of the public, having sold a plot of land to his neighbour, informs him that he had been a member of the home guard during the war. The best bit must have been when he added that he'd buried a box of bombs in that plot at the end of the war.

Somewhat curious, and no doubt concerned at his new acquisition, the new owner scrapes away the earth to discover a rusty metal plate painted with the words 'Albright & Wilson'. Scraping away some more earth, he exposes what looks like bottle tops. At this point he calls the police.

Even before I arrive, I am pretty sure of what this amounts to. The 'A & W' metal plate would normally be found on the inside of the lid, so the original wooden container has completely disintegrated. During the war, Albright and Wilson manufactured what were called SIP grenades, i.e. Self Igniting

Phosphorous. These babies are glass bottles that have been filled with benzene and white phosphorous with a rubber strip added to gelatinise the benzene. The idea is to hurl the thing at an approaching vehicle or fire it from a projector. The glass would shatter and the phosphorous, on contact with the air, would ignite. The benzene would also ignite – and bingo! It is a kind of Molotov cocktail.

Being glass, they are not easily handled or stored and if air gets into the mix, either through a crack in the bottle or through a rusted crown cork, well, curtains! Fortunately, no one had put a spade through any of them in the thirty years they had lain there minding their own business.

So it is down to me to scrape away the earth and gingerly lift each out of their resting place into a bucket of water. This will ensure that the air stays excluded. There are two layers: thirty-six bottles in total. I carry them to the middle of a nearby field and destroy them in a controlled explosion with a length of detonating cord. We spend an hour afterwards raking the soil to burn off the remaining phosphorous – nasty horrible sticky stuff, which we have to be very careful does not contaminate our boots, clothes or skin.

Because we do a relatively dangerous job, some people must think Ammo Techs have an in-built death wish and, therefore, won't mind doing any other dangerous job that comes along. This can be the only reason why I was 'spammed'

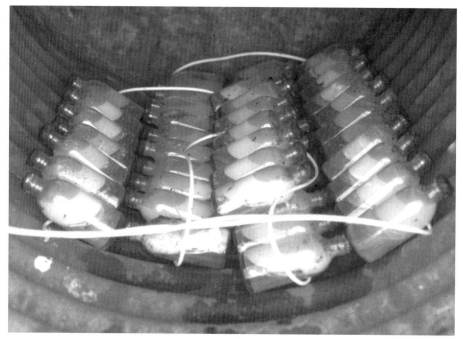

Above: Contained in a large wriggly tin drum and wrapped in detonating cord, the glass grenades await execution.

to do a job of work for the civilian proof establishment at Shoeburyness, where a trial was being carried out on 66mm HE anti-tank rockets. It was feared that if a pallet of rockets was dropped by accident from a reasonable height, the fuzes might arm. The trial, therefore, was to drop such a pallet and then X-ray each of the rocket fuzes to ensure that the safety in storage mechanism worked.

After each dropped pallet, I'm sent in with a Stanley knife to extricate a container, cut away the cardboard packaging and free up each missile. Ever so carefully, I would then manhandle it under X-ray equipment that someone else could operate from a safe distance away, behind a concrete wall. Once X-rayed I would then repeat the exercise. I mean, let's face it, anyone could have done that bloody job. It didn't need a technician, did it? Ammo Techs, I begin to understand, are very cost effective!

Following my stint at Shoeburyness, I am called to investigate a couple of accidents that involved ammunition, one of which requires a little bit of detective work to solve. The Royal Military Police come to see me the afternoon after one accident and explains what they know. A group of new army recruits has been participating in a map reading exercise on the Thetford training area in Norfolk. Afterwards, as the soldiers jump down from the back of a truck at Bodney Camp, there is a substantial crack – an explosion. A number of lads are injured and hospitalised and one lad undergoes surgery on a serious leg injury.

The RMP show me a glass phial, which contains bloodied pieces of brass that have been removed from the soldier with the leg injury. Most of the bits look like small arms ammunition and their opinion is that the recruits have been discovering and collecting up discarded cartridge cases; one such cartridge was live and had, in some way, functioned. Frankly, this is unlikely and, looking closer at the phial, I can see that one piece of distorted frag' does not originate from small arms ammunition. My suspicions are aroused.

I drive out to Bodney Camp to inspect the scene of the explosion. On the hard standing where the soldiers had debussed, there is nothing obvious to see because, with the explosion occurring off the ground, there is no crater. However, examining an adjacent wall, I find bits of spring and cogs that had obviously struck the wall and dropped to the floor. This tells me that some form of fuzing has been involved in the explosion. On a map, their platoon sergeant shows me the route the recruits had been given for their exercise and, when I see that it crossed the impact area of an anti-tank range, I know I have it.

I return to Colchester and refer to the Ammunition and Explosive Regulations manuals, which had persecuted me at Chepstow, but were now the equivalent of a bible. I scan through the different types of ammunition, concentrating on anti-tank natures and eventually come to my friend the 66mm anti-tank rocket: the same ammunition I had decanted from pallets at the P&EE some months before. This rocket is a portable self-contained round of ammunition that allows an infantry man to engage an armoured vehicle up to about 300 metres and punch a hole in it. Looking at a picture of the fuzing mechanism, I soon identify the large fragment as the detonator holder. This fuze normally functions on impact, but it also contains what is called a graze action. In other words, the fuze should still function even if it only grazes the target. It was this aspect that the Proof and Experimental establishment at Shoeburyness had been so concerned about.

The Bodney Camp incident was then easy to deduce. Some months previously, a rocket had been fired during target practice. The warhead hadn't functioned for some reason, but the impact had separated the fuze from the warhead. I know this because if it hadn't separated and the lad had picked that up as well, he would have been blown to bits – along with his mates. So, the lad had found this small, innocuous, silver object lying in the grass and placed it in his pocket together with the brass small arms cases he had been collecting. The fuze, however, was armed and had been since a millisecond or two after the rocket had been fired. Jumping out of the truck was sufficient to cause a locking bar to move, which allowed the spring loaded striker to plunge into the detonator – and bang! His injuries were consistent with about 5gm of an azide type of high explosive.

The next day, I visit the lad in hospital. With his little finger now missing and a large hole in upper thigh he is, understandably, feeling quite sorry for himself. Having been told at the beginning of the exercise not to pick up any strange objects, he is also sticking to a story that he has only recovered empty cartridge cases. Presented with the evidence and a picture of the item, however, he eventually admits to removing it from the range. Frankly, he is lucky to be alive and, considering the proximity of his pocket, he can at least console himself that his injuries might have been far worse!

It is around this time that there is a poignant event, when I am tasked to be on hand during the launch of a military vessel at Lowestoft. Chatting to a security man at the yard there, I discover that he is Cal Brown's father in law. Cal had been the No. 2 in the Bessbrook team, which was wiped out in 1975 – surely, an amazing coincidence. The family kindly invites me to lunch and shows me Cal's grave at nearby Lound. Jen also knew Cal from our Kineton days and we are able to lay flowers on his grave at the Remembrance service later that year.

Selected for promotion that year, I only serve with the Ammunition Inspectorate for a short time. I did, however, really enjoy it. The only niggle was the oversight of IEDD work, which I felt could be unreasonable at times and occasionally oppressive. For example I was called to a cottage in Suffolk where a lady had received an envelope with an Irish post mark on it. Terrorist outrages in cities were frequently seen on television at this time, so she called the police.

In accordance with their procedures, they notified the Joint EOD Reporting Centre who, having received such a request, tasked me as the area duty operator.

I arrive, take one look at the envelope, and immediately see that it doesn't contain a device – too light and thin. In fact, it contains Irish tote tickets. Later, I get grilled by the headquarters on why I hadn't X-rayed the package or taken it more seriously. Some people haven't got enough to do! It seems that because nice Mrs Pomfret from a backwater village in Suffolk considered herself a target for the PIRA, then apparently so should I!

Directorate of Land Service Ammunition — Proof Branch – 1979

In 1977 I'm posted to a Forward Ammunition Unit at Paderborn in Germany as a staff sergeant. Two years later, I'm again promoted and posted back to the UK as a warrant officer, class 2. This time it is to Proof Branch of the MoD Directorate of Land Service Ammunition at Didcot in Oxfordshire. Didcot is where the British Army's most important wartime commodity is managed.

The task of Proof Branch is to `prove` the quality of ammunition. This involves organising the selection of ammunition from the depots, maintaining a consistent temperature for the propelling charges at the range, capturing the muzzle velocities as they are fired and also plotting the fall of shot at the sharp end. It's quite amazing; for if you stand watching artillery pieces firing for any length of time, you can eventually spot the shells exiting the muzzle. They look like elongated black darts. Having, on one occasion, got used to shells fired with a super charge, when they were then fired with a normal charge I swear I could almost read their lot number stencilled on the body!

Following our work, civil servants back at Didcot (of the boffin variety) would analyse the data and calculate the quality of the ammunition. Stan Twine was the well-respected subject matter expert and top number cruncher during my time there. With his long, grey hair and scientific outlook, the troops often didn't know what to make of him!

Most of our work is carried out at the ranges at either Salisbury Plain or in Germany. I did manage, however, to negotiate myself a Proof in Belize in Central America and, in December 1980, I fell for a trip to Hong Kong which is where I first heard that John Lennon had been shot. Both Proofs were to check the quality of the operational 81mm HE mortar bomb stocks stored there.

The most notable thing about the proof in Belize is that the mortar base plates just keep bedding into the soft ground until only 6 inches of the tube protrudes from the ground. This is not much good if the mortar has been used at operational rates and/or you have to retreat in a hurry. I always wondered how they got on with this weapon in the Falklands War.

With regard to the trip to Belize, it is the temperature and humidity that comes as a shock to the system. As you step out of the plane it envelopes you and I don't stop sweating until the day I step back onto the plane. Even washing a pair of socks in the morning and hanging them out to dry doesn't work because, by the evening, they are still soaking wet due to the high humidity. Like everyone else, I carry two full water bottles on my hips, but one of these would always be drunk by the time I'd walked to the helicopter pad.

Another major challenge for me are the land crabs, which are about 10 inches across. I nearly have a heart attack when I go to pick up a piece of equipment and one nearly takes my finger off with its large fighting claw.

During our trip to Belize the Warrant Officer Ammo Tech, Frank Smith, is on leave. As a consequence, as I step off the plane, the police are waiting and politely ask if I will deal with a bomb someone has handed in at the local police station. Well, they ask so nicely – what can I say?

The object is about 10 inches long and 6 inches in diameter, and made of a rigid form of canvas. With no equipment available to me, it could have been awkward. Anyway, I tentatively slit open the tube with a knife to confirm that there is no switching arrangement present; however, there is electrical wiring and an electrical igniter (i.e. squib) in place. The tube is packed with a magnesium powder, which I assume to be explosive, and I separate out all the components – job done!

A year or two later, I discovered that the object had probably been a special effect from the film *Dogs of War*, which had been shot in Belize a year or so before!

Proof Branch is almost certainly one of the most enjoyable jobs I ever have in my career as an Ammo Tech. It is from here, however, that I am nominated for my third tour of duty in Northern Ireland.

3RD TOUR NI — 1981

The high octane of the GPO sorting office and Antrim mortar incidents had receded into mere memory when, four years after my last operational tour, I am earmarked for my second and final tour of duty as an operator. What goes around comes around, as they say, and this time it is to lead the section based in the little village of Bessbrook. It is my job to provide cover for all the explosive-related incidents and support SF operations across the 'bandit country' of South Armagh. South Armagh, by this time, has gained a reputation all of its own.

In the intervening period, my wife gives birth to our two eldest children and the conflict in Ireland has become something of a backdrop to the day job. The subject, however, is often on the agenda at regimental dinner nights, whenever the 'lamps get swung' – which is probably too often, as I'm sure our long-suffering and bored 'wags' would attest.

We are all aware that 1981 is not on the same scale as the early seventies, but it is still a time of high activity on both the political and military fronts. A series of high-profile hunger strikes begin in 1981, which result in the deaths of ten Republican prisoners. Not winning any concessions from the British Government for this strategy, a new realism is spawned and the green shoots of a political solution begin to be seen from there on in. 1981 is also the last big year for PIRA bombings and shootings. After this, the statistics show that this type of violence tails off, gradually, year by year and I am proud to say that my team and I did what we could to thwart PIRA's operational aspirations in that green and deadly land. Given a fair crack, we helped unravel and spoil their set pieces and made them safe, or at the very least we cleared away their highly hazardous scrap.

In this, my third and final tour of duty in Ulster, I serve alongside soldiers of the 1st Battalion the Queen's Lancashire Regiment (the old Loyals Regiment from Preston that had my mate sweeping the road!) and then the 1st Battalion the Royal Green Jackets: two fine infantry regiments. There are also the men and women of the Ulster Defence Regiment (UDR) and Royal Ulster Constabulary (RUC) whom I found to be extremely decent, cheerful people doing their best in a nightmare situation, caught, as they were, between religious rocks and hard politics. We are supported by the Royal Engineer Specialist Search Teams (REST) and RMP Weapons Intelligence Section (WIS), whose expertise I rely upon to keep me alive. The camaraderie everyone feels for each other; well, at times, you can almost touch it. This is the antithesis of what we feel for our secret, ruthless and technically advanced enemy, who are so bound up trying to kill us. Such is the nature of war, because for all of us who served in Northern Ireland, and especially those who served in South Armagh, that's exactly what it felt like.

18th January 1981
The Lie of the Land

Politically, Ulster has always been a fractious place and, for twelve years or so, it has been at war with itself. This time around the bullet is accompanied by extensive use of the bomb: the Improvised Explosive Device (IED). Prolific use of explosives is intended to bring the Province to its knees. It won't happen because, for any government, there is too much at stake, but you can't tell PIRA that. To date, fifteen IED operators had been killed. Because the teams aren't exempt from any other threats that face security forces, in 1979 an IEDD team had been ambushed on the way back from an incident and the second vehicle blown up. This resulted in the death of the team's signalman and his military escort.

Prior to Northern Ireland, our people walked up to IEDs in Borneo, Aden, Cyprus and also Hong Kong. This campaign, however, is on a different scale to all that went before. For our survival, we have had to up our game. Every day you will look in the mirror and wonder if there's a dragon out there that's luckier than you.

I walk through Aldergrove Airport into the arrivals area. At the Military Movements desk one young guy in civvies holds up a card on which is written '321'. I head for him and introduce myself. 'WO2 Wharton – are you waiting for me?' He is. We shake hands and he introduces himself as a lance corporal from the headquarters at Lisburn. I follow him to the airport café where two guys sit. One is a military escort, the other I recognise as a Staff Sergeant Ammunition Technician with whom I've served before. He's flown in from Germany and he's heading for the Belfast Section. I tell him I'm headed for the ATO Section at Bessbrook near Newry, but he already knows. He and I have different types of battle to fight. His is shift work: fast and furious – quick responses that befit the protection of a city. The *modus operandi* for me is different: occasionally fast and furious, but mainly slow and unhurried since, in the countryside, terrorists have plenty of time and space to set up attacks. Only second tour operators serve there now. In South Armagh, it is the unpicking of each puzzle that is the challenge; often what you see and hear is what they want you to see and hear. It may only be a few miles square, but PIRA always has something on the go there. In South Armagh a gung-ho attitude to the work can and will quickly become a liability for everyone concerned.

The drive out of the airport is convoluted, through various checkpoints and security points. For me, though, the first hint that normality really doesn't live here is that I see British Police Officers in flack jackets carrying both automatic rifles and pistols as a matter of routine. I accept that this type of policing is pretty much an anathema to the desires of the British people, but each time I come here I do find it oddly disturbing. But what's the alternative when invisible men are bent on killing you? For my money, these coppers, and the members of the local Ulster Defence Regiment, all of whom live on the civilian net, have to be the most courageous of all the SF.

As we travel, there's nothing visible about us to say that we're army, but it's probably obvious to anyone who might be clocking us and our driver doesn't hang about, even though the area we're travelling through is considered safe, i.e. it is predominantly Unionist. Having said that, the province is only 60 miles by 80 (about the size of Yorkshire and Humberside together); nowhere is really outside the reach of this enemy, which is integrated into the populace and doesn't wear a uniform.

Whilst there are many terrorist splinter groups operating across the Province, by far the most ambitious in their operations and the most technically competent are the Provisional IRA. We've come a long way in our knowledge of Improvised Explosive Devices and how they can be deployed – because so have they.

As the landscape flashes past I think of those who have gone before me. It's

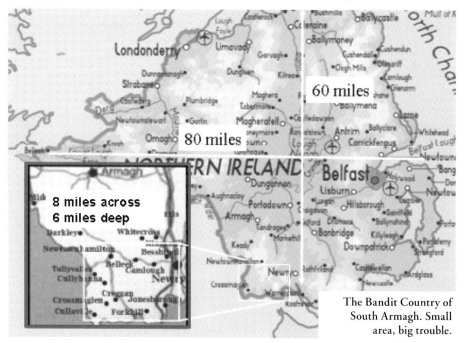

The Bandit Country of South Armagh. Small area, big trouble.

ten years since the first IEDD operator was killed. I knew a number of them. They are our fallen; never to grow old; frozen forever into the space and time of our last meeting.

The drive to the British Army HQ at Lisburn takes about 20 minutes. On arrival, I see that HQ 321 EOD Company is still one portakabin complex among many. To date, the unit has investigated over 12,000 incidents involving explosives. Half were live devices and neutralised. Most people will think the statistics quite an achievement.

I eventually meet the unit chief clerk and fill in a form with questions like 'Have you made a will?' 'Next of kin?' My photograph is taken and it is this that will appear in the newspapers if I don't make it through. Eventually I'll have my fingerprints taken to eliminate them from any forensic evidence I submit. I'm then taken to the commanding officer's office and asked to take a seat.

Two senior RAOC officers oversee bomb disposal activities across the province. The first is the commanding officer of 321 EOD Company who is a major. This is unusual because a CO is normally a lieutenant colonel. This chap also holds an appointment called SATO, which is an abbreviation for Senior Ammunition Technical Officer. The second RAOC officer is a lieutenant colonel. He is the IEDD adviser to the General Officer Commanding (GOC) British Forces, NI. Whilst he doesn't have command responsibility for the unit, he holds the appointment of CATO (Chief ATO). From time to time he'll issue Standing Operating Procedures that are mandatory for everyone. If you're confused about who is actually running the ship then you'll just have to read the above for a second or third time.

From the SATO's office, I look out over the asphalt square that separates the 321 portakabin from the more substantial building, which is the British Army HQ. I then have just a few moments to contemplate the guy writing at his desk before he looks up at me with half a smile on his lips, like a dog just before it bites you. Let's call him JR. He welcomes me to 321. We know each other quite well as we've served together twice before. We also attended the same pre-operations IEDD course a couple of months before and it was there that he had sidled over to me to explain that if I should be thinking about medals, which I wasn't, then I should put it out of my mind because, as he put it, 'If the unit puts you up for an award you'll have to answer to me.' Now, I happen to think that any soldier is entitled to be affronted by that, especially as I gave him no justification for saying it. Me, well frankly, I was bemused. It was only when reflecting on it later that I realised I should have taken it more seriously. Anyway, I kind of laughed it off and let it go, so today I'm none the wiser as to his reasoning. In case anyone might think he has a sense of humour, then I will say to them that this guy doesn't have a reputation that stretches all that far in that direction. Watching him now, across the desk as he looks at me, I wonder if there's more of it to come.

Just a week before I was due to report for this tour of duty my father collapsed at home and died from a heart attack. He was fifty-four years old and so it came as a great shock to all of us. I was devastated by his loss. My father had no will and my mother didn't even have her own bank account at that time and so urgent financial arrangements had to be made. Probate matters, therefore, held up my deployment by a few days.

Two days after the funeral I report for duty. I'm probably still in shock. I don't get much sympathy, though. Instead, the SATO intimates that the delay in reporting has been a bit of a nuisance – a buggerance factor since the incumbent ATO at Bessbrook will have been inconvenienced, having had to stay on to cover for me. I'm a bit miffed by this because the guy is a mate of mine; I'm sure he was all right with it and, in any case, I would have done the same for him.

The SATO doesn't hang around and, in his own inimitable way, gets to the nub of it – the real ice breaker – 'I told them I don't think you are the right person for Bessbrook.' By 'them' I assume he's referring to the MoD Ammunition Headquarters at Didcot who staff up the NI Operator posts. For a second, I think he means that I may not cope with the tour because of my father's death, but then I realise he just thinks I'm not up to the job. It also becomes clear that he thinks I've been promoted to warrant officer too soon. Well he's entitled to all these opinions, I guess, but revealing his thoughts to me in this way isn't likely to get us very far up the positive scale.

I really wonder about what is going on in the SATO's head. Maybe he thinks I haven't got the nerve. Well I think I've already proved it. But who really knows where their threshold is? OK, I didn't score especially highly at the IEDD Pre-Ops Exercises. There was one particular mortar job I made a balls of! But I wouldn't be sitting here if the overall results had been too bad. Admittedly, I don't, in any way, profess to be an archetypical Bomb Disposal hero such as they are often dramatised by TV and films. Frankly, who does? I'm a fairly average bloke. I don't like heights much and I can't see the point of spiders. I've felt gut-churning fear and I can't say I like it. I certainly don't see myself as brave. I understand the risks and I've simply applied the techniques I've been taught the best I can. Like many of my contemporaries, I didn't volunteer to carry out this work; wasn't even told about it when I became an Ammo Tech. In the early days of the campaign the Ammunition Technicians who carried out these duties were not selected on whether they had an aptitude for it or not. Ammunition Technicians were a cross-section of types you might see in any profession, who

PRE-OPERATIONS IEDD EXERCISE 'COLD MEECE'

PIRA The Pre Ops course IEDD exercise is called Exercise Cold Meece. It's named after a village in Staffordshire near to where the exercise originated. The exercise is four days in duration and primarily designed to test operators and No 2s in a variety of bomb-related scenarios. The failure rate can be high. With a lack of any purpose-built facility, the exercise is set in an overgrown, derelict, MOD depot near Grantham. The tests can be taxing, not least because an operator has first to be able to imagine, for example, that the overgrown track he's standing on is the main street of a town, the crumbling concrete bunker with its smashed windows on his left is a hospital, and the water tower behind him is an oil refinery. The directing staff also have personal idiosyncrasies in terms of expectations.

The fear of booby traps can make you too cautious and anyone who fails to consider them sufficiently is penalised for being reckless. Sometimes you wonder how anyone gets through the course at all!

were given no choice if they wanted to remain Ammunition Technicians.

Anyway, the SATO gives me the spiel in terms of his expectations, but by now I'm distracted and various thoughts tumble around my mind. I'm thinking, rightly or wrongly, that this guy really doesn't like me and doesn't want me here. I'm also thinking that he has a reputation that precedes him among my brethren – metaphorically speaking, he doesn't take prisoners. We know that he's quite ruthless. So I begin to think of the small number of ATOs who have been replaced during the campaign. None to my knowledge went on to have successful careers as Ammunition Technicians; indeed, most had to change profession. All these thoughts make me distinctly uncomfortable. If the matter between us should get out of hand, it's likely to be dealt with quickly. We are in an operational theatre after all. No one has time to piss about. If push comes to shove, however, the system we're all signed up to tends to support those who have the seniority. It's part and parcel of the regimental system. This is how I see it anyway. The interview ends.

Fortunately, my first encounter with the CATO, Lt Col Chris Hendy, is a much more constructive affair – like normal. He's an upbeat sort of bloke, relaxed in his demeanour and personable, less complicated perhaps, and he doesn't have a reputation that precedes him. He has expectations of me, but doesn't have preconceived ideas as to my ability. I come away feeling he's supportive. Frankly, it's what I would have expected from any senior officer whose unit is carrying out seriously dangerous operations. But clearly what one expects isn't always what one gets!

In passing let me also say there has always been a tension between those two senior posts – perhaps it's healthy. The SATO, as the CO, has command of the unit, but the CATO, who is also located within the 321 HQ, sees himself as ultimately accountable to the GOC for the efficacy of the unit. It could be easy for the two appointments to get in each other's way and I suspect that, at times, they do.

With the initial introductions over, I'm expected to attend an induction course that will include intelligence and forensic briefings and also explosive demonstrations. I'll need to return to Lisburn for this at a later date, since today is Sunday and Headquarters NI is effectively shut. For now, though, at last, I'm on the final leg of my journey to Bessbrook Mill and it's another fast car ride.

Daylight has given way to darkness as the car speeds along. Only a black landscape and oncoming car headlights are discernible. They flash past in a blur and I hardly notice them. My mind is still fixed on the matter that is most likely to have consequences for me. I rationalise the situation, as you do, and a saying jumps into my mind – 'Life's a bitch and then you're dead'. I discount it. Life had been too good thus far to be messed up by someone else's prejudices. In my mind my priorities are clear: getting home and in one piece and doing a good job that I can be proud of. As I hadn't screwed up in my career just yet, here would be a bad place to start. In fact (and the thought kind of cheers me up), I'm quite looking forward to getting stuck in to the work. If the next four months are going to be a bitch, well, at least I'd be mentally prepared for it, I guess.

We arrive in the village of Bessbrook at about 7 p.m. and a few minutes later I get my first sight of the heavily fortified HQ, which I've heard a lot about but never yet seen.

HQ Bessbrook Mill

As with many old mills across the Province, Bessbrook Mill has been turned into a modern version of a fort. It's fenced in with sheets of wriggly tin. Ugly grey breeze block sentry posts, called sangars, have been erected at each entrance, and external walls are floodlit at night. The approach to the base has a chicane to prevent vehicle-borne bombs breaking through and there are strict drills to be followed in the event of a bomb or mortar attack. Across the way is the concreted helicopter port, which, according to the *Guinness Book of Records*, is the busiest in Europe.

Civilians who live nearby will be nervous, because we're a target seven days

Operational Headquarters for South Armagh with the busiest heli-port in Europe in the foreground.

a week and there is often collateral damage from PIRA's attacks. No one can afford to be complacent; the enemy is cunning and persistent, and despite the millions spent obtaining information, surprise is almost always on their side.

How it must be to live out your life and raise a family surrounded by this turmoil is impossible for us to imagine. Soldiers are like tourists; we fly in and a few months later we're out again, back to the relative calm of the mainland. We live in a bubble, separated from the populace, but outside of the Mill they go about their business the best they can and, because the mayhem has been ongoing for so long, everyone in the province will have been touched by it in one way or another.

The Mill contains, I guess, about 600 soldiers: infantry, plus a number of supporting echelons like signalmen, search teams, Army Air Corps, logistics and technicians, cooks and intelligence people, police liaison officers. There are probably other specialists that I don't even know about. The regiment has detachments based at Crossmaglen and Newtownhamilton and is supported by another regiment who have a company based at Forkhill. It's quite a lot of soldiers to cover such a relatively small area and it is my job to provide specialist IEDD support and advice to all those units and the police as they each carry out their anti-terrorist operations.

Due to the very high probability of attack from ambush bombs, pretty much all roads south of Newry are out of bounds to green vehicles. Most of the jobs I'll be tasked to will be planned in advance, involve helicopter sorties and kick off as dawn breaks. Some will be high-adrenalin races against time, but those are likely to be in the minority.

I have a team office and our sleeping accommodation is attached. In fact, each member of the team has his own room. As the ATO section has been here since the beginning, we're fairly comfortable. There's a sofa, soft chairs, TV, video machine, coffee making facilities and a fridge; our facilities are looked on

WHEELBARROW

The Remote Control Vehicle (RCV) Wheelbarrow is the workhorse developed by the MOD in double quick time to provide operators with a remote IEDD capability. It's highly versatile as it can carry a variety of equipments, specialist explosives and weapons that can be deployed against anything really. Its main limitations are the two car batteries it is powered by, which can run out of power when the RCV is at the sharp end, the 100m umbilical cord that too easily gets trapped or chopped and, despite the tracks, an inability to operate on soft ground.

enviously by the regiments that come and go. We even have a technological miracle provided by the *Sun* newspaper's latest 'Support the Troops' campaign. It's a games console where the combatants can use a TV screen to play ping pong. It's very popular. Who can say what it'll lead to?

A large map on the wall shows the boundary of our tactical area of responsibility. The map is peppered with colour-coded map pins; each pin is a job; each colour depicts whether a job turned out to be a hoax, false alarm, live device, incendiary, explosion or a find. This is how we categorise the outcome of each IEDD task.

With more equipment than most other teams to operate and maintain, I have a second No. 2. So there are four of us in the team – a corporal Ammunition Technician,

Whelbarrow, the Complete Equipment Schedule.

a lance corporal driver and a Royal Signals, Electronic Counter Measures (ECM) Operator, who we affectionately call 'Bleep'. One other, shall we say, more mechanical member of the team is the Remote Control Vehicle (RCV), 'Wheelbarrow Mk. 6'. Wheelbarrow can be expected to take many more risks than I ever will.

At the end of the four months I'll be replaced by another second tour operator. The other members of the team will also turnover at the end of their four months. This gradual turnover is called roulement. The infantry units, however, are replaced en masse at the end of their tour.

As I follow the driver through the corridor complex, an infantry officer, a captain, approaches and my driver introduces me. He's the regiment's adjutant. He smiles broadly, 'Welcome to Bessbrook, Felix. Good to have you onboard.' He calls me Felix because that's the radio code name for the ATO. 321 vehicles, have a cat's face emblazoned on them.

He continues, 'Get an early night as we've a body on the border and you're going out at first light.'

It's a bit of a shock.

At the office, I meet the outgoing ATO, Steve Wilks, and the team and I get introduced. I'm briefed on tomorrow's job. Eventually, I get some sleep.

19th January 1981

The Body

A dirty war played out for the highest stakes.

Shortly after dawn, the outgoing ATO, the team and I, are taken by helicopter to the border near Jonesborough, and we set about the grisly work of recovering the body. The job is made a little easier for us only because he's a member of the Provisional IRA. I'm told he's an informer who's been executed. It seems that the Security Forces received information recently, which led to the recovery of a large explosives cache in County Down. It looks as if he's been fingered for it. He was twenty-four years old.

One dark night, hard men abducted him from his house in Belfast. It isn't hard to imagine the fear he must have felt as he was manhandled away to his doom, probably to a lonely farm somewhere near the border. He's interrogated to get a confession and eventually executed with a series of pistol shots. His duffle coat is buttoned up, presumably to keep him together for transportation to the border. He's thrown down and, for good measure, shots are fired into the back of his head with an ArmaLite Rifle. It's the PIRA mark of a 'tout'. He lies now on a muddy bank a few hundred yards from the border. He's the 170th person to die in South Armagh as a result of the conflict. South Armagh is dubbed 'bandit country' by the Security Forces for good reason.

NUMBER ONE SEVEN ZERO

The day you swore the cause,
you never thought you'd end up here
despising the knocks that fed your fear.
And when they came those ghosts in grey
and bundled you off, took you away
they already knew that you had sold
your pitiful soul for British gold.

Release is not easy from their evil spell
so come, accept the kiss of death.
Don't speak, listen, save your breath.
It's over my friend, there's nowhere to run
so allow your tormentors their bit of fun.
Don't panic, don't even try to resist,
ignore the wires that cut into your wrists.

The darkened room, the glowing light.
Scream, scream no one can hear you cry,
Thud, thud, says the pistol, I release you to die.
Rat, tat, tat, those flashes in the Armagh night
smack the hollow kiss of the ArmaLite.

In death there's a kind of peace around
as muddied you lie there all alone,
'ourselves', well, they have crept off home.
Those ghosts have left with ne'er a trace,
time only to spit on the man with no face.

We'll take you home now to your kith and kin,
I know not, but perhaps you were a friend,
supported my cause that brought your end.
But by double crossing the battle lines,
you're now a sad statistic of these troubled times.

January 1981

In case his body is booby trapped, we use the Wheelbarrow to pull him along the road a short distance and away from the immediate area. The ground is searched but nothing untoward is found.

I stand over the guy. His hands are bound with metal wire and he's a bloody mess. This is not the first body I've stood over, but it's the first time I've seen someone's brains; they're in the road. It's a sad, sickening end to anybody's life. It's also a sobering reintroduction for me into the brutality of the 'Irish troubles' and a timely reminder, if ever I needed it, that for PIRA, the Security Forces and especially the Ulster people, this is being played out for the highest stakes.

From the Passive to the Offensive

We're back from the border by lunchtime and the outgoing ATO and I begin the handover in earnest. Quite naturally, since he wants to get home! We walk the Mill and I'm introduced to some of the key people I'll be working with: the infantry Ops Staff, RUC Liaison Officers, Heli Operations, intelligence people, the Royal Engineer Search Team leader; each an expert in his own field and a more cheerful bunch of blokes I have yet to meet.

All of our team equipment, weapons and explosives have to be accounted for and signed off. My next port of call is therefore the explosives store. I survey the explosive materials we have at our disposal: plastic explosives, sheet explosives, cutting charges, Disrupter cartridges. There's even a variety of 12-bore shotgun cartridges. It's a far cry from what I would have been looking at just a few years ago.

For anyone in the proximity of a high-order detonation, the effect on the human body is usually catastrophic – shattering. When the dragon roars, the effect is instantaneous: a 'crack' of a sound, not a 'boom'. The white hot gas and heat are expanding at 4,000 metres a second. There isn't time to duck or leap out of the way; no time for evasive action. Anything that can be moved by the blast will be. Anything that will shatter or fragment will. Anything that can be ripped off is. Those that have survived the dragon's breath describe it as a white light. If you are far enough away from it, the bomb disposal operator's suit will deflect it, but if you are too close nothing can save you, for what can shatter metal easily shreds flesh, bone and sinew.

Ways have now been developed to utilise those same explosive effects against improvised devices. There's some history and philosophy around IEDD techniques and equipment so it's probably worth explaining it now. An often touted and perhaps traditional view of a bomb disposal operator is of an eccentric, but cool head, with a steady hand and a briefcase containing various tools: two of which must be a stethoscope and a pair of wire cutters. If this is the picture you have in your head, well it's not too far off the mark should you reflect back to 1966/67. I emphasise 1966/67 because this was a hectic time for Ammunition Technicians serving in Hong Kong. Most people today probably don't realise that Communist elements within Hong Kong tried to destabilise the province in that year with multiple attacks of crude Improvised Explosive Devices. Ammunition Technicians worked with the Hong Kong police to counter these attacks and thousands of devices were dealt with. Whilst a number of operators were injured in the Hong Kong Campaign, it is quite amazing that we lost only one – Sergeant Charles Workman. He bled to death on a ledge after being blown over a cliff by the force of an explosion. The survival rate was higher in Hong Kong partly because the bomb makers used only gunpowders, or low explosives as they're called, rather than high explosives like Semtex, TNT and PETN.

Back to our stereotype; whilst any assumed ability to provide a steady hand is questionable and no one would argue that anyone doing this job is eccentric, by 1966, operators did have a much bigger box of tricks to play with than simply a set of tools in a satchel or a briefcase. More advanced tools, however, didn't necessarily make the job any safer. For example, an operator could call upon an electronic stethoscope so sensitive that placed on a wooden box it could detect the tick of a good watch. This question was asked by an over-enthusiastic student: 'If it is so sensitive to sound, should the bomb go off, wouldn't the noise make you deaf?'

Another key component is glue. Because an operator would want to limit any movement of the device, he would first secure (i.e. glue) the suspect package to the ground. For this, he used a urethane foam called Coolag. This adhesive is formed by mixing two agents that, when brought together, foam and then quickly solidify. Once the device is stuck fast he can use a plasma arc torch to produce an intense but localised heat from a 20,000 volt electrical charge. This could cut through thin metal-cased packages. There is even a way to attach the equipment to the package and it would then trepan a hole in it remotely. Following this, liquid nitrogen is available to be pumped into the package via the hole, which freezes batteries, stops clockwork mechanisms and solidifies any other moving parts. If the bomb has not gone off at this point in the proceedings and you are, therefore, still around, you might now be in a good position to snip away at the key components. It is at this point that the legendary wire cutters come into their own.

Other major developments in the field include an armoured screen on wheels that could be pushed to the target, keeping the screen between the device and the operator. With this in place, a long-handled shovel pushed through a hole can be used to manipulate and even lift the device away from the intended target. I know all this because this was the equipment I was taught to use at my first IEDD course in 1970. At the time, I have to say, it all seemed rather reasonable and quite exciting.

The shortcomings of all the IEDD equipment in those days can be summarised as passive, less than offensive in nature and time-consuming to deploy. This is not to mention the number of times the device has to be approached by the operator. We used up time trying to confirm whether a device was actually real or not and then spent an awful lot of time in the danger area. These inadequate Render Safe strategies, together with this perverse way of thinking, were initially carried forward into the NI Campaign.

A big difference between the Hong Kong emergency and the NI campaign was not least the significant amounts and types of explosives the NI terrorists had access to. Another was the technology available to PIRA. British Telecom components discovered in early Irish devices and the sophistication in the types of switching used suggested that technicians with a BT-type background were building them. The device circuitry was also often complex, incorporating multiple switching arrangements. Sometimes what the operator could easily get his hands on is what they wanted him to touch, move or cut.

The more passive approach to IEDD almost certainly contributed to the death of the first Operator, Capt. Stewardson. He attempted to gain access to a plywood container (via the lid) after having secured the device to the ground using the Coolag mixture. X-rays taken of similar devices later showed that a clever method of switching had been used by the bomber. Cutting into devices by hand, and chopping wires as an initial action, quickly became a no-no. Even so, the passive approach to dealing with devices was perpetuated. When, for example, it was discovered that detergent foam could disperse the fireball and heat from an explosion, thereby significantly reducing the blast effects, an armoured Humber vehicle (called a Pig) was adapted to dispense foam over devices. This technique was especially used in Belfast from 1973 through to 1977, mainly to combat car bombs. Whilst there is no doubt it worked when it worked; when it didn't work (because, for example, the bomb didn't function or it was a false alarm), the whole city was tied up for hours and hours. And if, as happened at least once, an operator made a manual approach into the foam, he could become completely disorientated in the white-out and lost, which is a bit disconcerting when you assume you are in the vicinity of a large car bomb.

Another piece of kit was put forward by the BBC *World in Action* team. They came to the Army School of Ammunition, when it was located at Bramley in Hampshire, to test out a specialist blanket that someone had invented. It was supposed to be capable of suppressing an explosive blast. As the slow motion cameras demonstrated, it could, more or less, but, as was pointed out at the time, the main problem with this idea is that someone has to place the blanket on the device in the first place and, if the device doesn't go off, someone has to lift it off – any volunteers? Some people must think this is what operators are paid to do!

We also have a range of equipment for accessing cars. I remember one of my earlier IEDD courses where the training area was littered with derelict cars on which operators practised their access techniques. We had a special punch that,

The Foaming Pig in action.
Belfast circa 1974.

when pressed against the windscreen could shatter it – a technique for removing windscreens all in one piece – and a type of can opener with which car body panels could be opened up like a tin of beans. I mean, it was good fun wrecking cars during courses, but it wasn't quite as funny using the techniques for real.

Portable X-ray machines were also quickly developed, which also perpetuated the passive approach. But these X-Ray equipments were not small and an early design required two men to lift them to the target – any volunteers? In the interim, operators were provided with what we called the 'Gamma Bomb'. Placing this 30 lb lump of lead in front of the device and opening it up at the front exposed an iridium radioactive source that emitted gamma rays. These have the same effect on film as X-rays and would provide us with a similar picture of the contents. The risks associated with radioactive materials, however, were real, and one more thing that can be added to the list that will probably jeopardise the health of some operators in the years to come.

The deployment of many of these pieces of equipment overlapped, so it's difficult to say now exactly when the policy changed to much more offensive IEDD techniques. In fact, even in the early days, as a form of self-preservation, I guess, operators were beginning to use home-made explosive strips and explosive charges to gain access to devices. It makes me shudder today, but I once read the SATO's comments in an IEDD report from that time, which required the operator to think seriously about sandbagging a device to reduce the likelihood of collateral damage occurring should the device function whilst he was taking that type of IEDD action!

I'm glad to say things had moved on by the time I carried out my first tour as an Operator in 1975. 'Disruption' became the byword for IEDD and this is now synonymous with the term 'controlled explosion' that everyone hears about. The applied principle is: why waste time and sweat trying to confirm if something is a device or not, thereby endangering yourself and providing the device with space in which to function? Get in quickly and do something about it immediately. If it turns out not to have been a device, well, so what? If you can reduce its effect – great. The most important thing is that any people at risk are evacuated and kept safe.

IEDD weaponry these days is capable of smashing electrical circuits before the explosives can be initiated. At the same time, the penetrative and disruptive effects of these weapons expose and, thereby, provide access to the device components. Some of the weapons are so extreme they have, as yet, not been approved for use on the UK mainland.

In 1974, we had what was called the Beguine: a heavy 8 x 10 inch square metal plate, which was projected at the device in the vertical plane by a high explosive charge. The plate was held in a wooden cassette fitted to a lightweight metal frame that could be deployed with the Wheelbarrow. Trouble was, it could easily be tangled up in the cables and the plate was often deflected. If that wasn't violent enough, we were issued with an 84mm Carl Gustav anti-tank gun: a weapon which is primarily designed to take out a main battle tank. Normally fired from the shoulder, when deployed for IEDD purposes, it was fitted in a stand. Solid non-high explosive rounds were fired to disrupt vehicle-borne devices. As mentioned earlier, I used the equipment in 1976, firing two rounds at a truck full of mortars. It was a bloody dangerous tool, not least because a projectile like that isn't easily stopped by the cab of a truck! The thinking behind its use is clearly a long way along the road from Hong Kong.

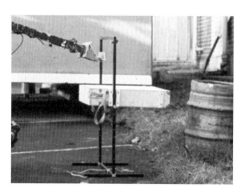

Left: Flatsword, second to none for sledging milkchurns and beer kegs.

Right: Pigstick, second to none for sledging packages.

Vehicle disruption became the name of the game.
A spinning beer keg spews out its lethal guts.

Above: Opening it all up in one go is only the beginning for the Operator...

Left: 84mm Anti Tank Gun Carl Gustav. I'm lining up the bore sight on the Leyland truck full of mortars. Authorised for use, this weapon was a desperate attempt to introduce something that could deal quickly with vehicle borne bombs.

22nd January 1981

Hoax, Monaghan Street, Newry

The outgoing ATO has left and, having been given a few days to settle in, at 9 a.m. I'm tasked to deal with an incident at a garage in Monaghan Street. A milk churn with a plastic bag taped around the rim has been discovered by the key holder of a garage. I send in the Wheelbarrow.

One shot with a Disrupter into the opening reveals that it's a hoax device comprised of an alarm clock, some wiring and a lump of putty. It's all been very straightforward for us. I declare the device clear and everything around quickly gets back to normal.

We'll never know the ulterior motive for wasting our time. One theory is that they want to know our patterns, so they are observing us/me.

A Hoax. Why?
For what reason?

Hoax components.
Putting the frighteners on somebody or perhaps they're clocking us.

23rd January 1981

Beer Keg Device, Belfast to Dundalk Railway Line

The next day I'm in a chopper and, when it banks steeply, I'm able to get a good look at the main Belfast to Dundalk railway line in the vicinity of Newtown. The railway is closed after a call to the Samaritans has said there are three devices on the railway line. A beer keg has since been spotted lying between the tracks. The helicopter pilot speaks to me. He's convinced that a Guinness barrel has fallen off a train. I don't share his thought. I mean, how many barrels of beer fall off trains? Isn't it every bloke's unrequited dream?

Beer kegs, like milk churns, are often used by PIRA in their explosive devices so there's a job for us here. The railway won't open again until it's cleared.

Left: An unpainted face can be a real give away so camouflage cream is mandatory in the Border Areas.

Right: All our equipments, including two of our vehicles are heli-portable. It's the safest way to get around South Armagh.

Above: The beer keg device. It isn't just about the device you can see…

Left: Agreeing tactics with the 1QLR Company Commander Major Scrace. 'Magic' a member of WIS is in the foreground.

Right: Eyeballing the beer keg from a relatively safe distance prior to rendering it safe. 60lbs of home made explosives would have made a real mess of the railway.

Left: 3 Brigade, ATO Section, Bessbrook. The job is all about teamwork. A great lineup and I probably never really thanked them enough. L to R Turner, Walker, Wharton, Wicks

There's a lot to think about at an incident, not least because the operator is also responsible for everyone else's safety. In the first place, there's a need to get a grip on the scenario and untangle it. Magic is most helpful at times like these, because an early all-important question is: what might the terrorist want to achieve by this attack? This exercise provides a list of likely options and combinations, which, depending on your imagination, can be very long or very short. By weighing the probabilities of each, you are better placed to manage the inherent risks. It is, therefore, important to get as much information as possible on how the incident materialised. In this case, however, there isn't any additional information except that every so often PIRA attack the railway and the bridges for which they're guaranteed publicity. The lack of information and the time the terrorist might have taken to plan it means we do have to be very careful, since the list of options might be considered long.

The Infantry make the area secure and the Royal Engineers carry out their searches. Eventually, we get on the ground. I need to eyeball the device, so, taking the binoculars, I scramble up the grassy bank over the fence into the adjacent field. Moving closer using the ground as cover, I get to within 30–40 metres of it. With the binoculars, I can see clearly that the top of the keg has been machined open and a plastic fertiliser sack is stuffed into the opening. A plywood Time and Power Unit (TPU) is lying next to the keg. The TPU provides the bomber with safety in arming and a time delay before the device functions. PIRA have come a long way since 1973 when thirty-eight of their operatives blew themselves up with their own bombs. Such a timer would normally have only a couple of hours to run, max, so it looks as if the device has failed to function. Tracing the electrical leads, I can see that a detonator is taped to the white detonating cord (or det cord, as we call it), which is protruding from the centre of the keg. The layman might think this is plastic clothes line, but it contains a core of high explosive and is used extensively in demolitions or quarrying for linking explosives together.

So is the device safe? Well, let's think about it. We might assume the bomber tested the batteries before he set out. If not, they could be flat. But perhaps the electrical contacts are contaminated. If so, a speck of dust or corrosion might be holding them fractionally apart. The smallest jolt is all that's needed for the circuit to close and the device to function. It's also hazardous because static electricity has been known to initiate electrical detonators and here we have the electrical leads almost touching the batteries.

I pass a soldier who has been far closer to the device than was good for him. He tells me he thinks it's a dud. I thank him for his intuition and advice!

Three devices were reported, but this information can be taken with a hefty pinch of salt. There are any number of possibilities to consider; one of which is that the keg is, in fact, a decoy and the real device is hidden somewhere else in the vicinity. Another is that the keg doesn't actually have a timer at all, but something more sinister; perhaps it's radio controlled. I'm thinking of multiple scenarios and the likelihood of each as I crawl away from the grassy bank and make my way back to the control point.

I have the RCV Wheelbarrow slung under a Wessex helicopter and the pilot lifts it from the field down in between the tracks. We also lift our heli-portable vehicle onto the tracks to provide us with some cover. The RCV is then tooled up with two IEDD Disrupters and the Browning semi-automatic shotgun. The latter is loaded with a mixture of shot. The Disrupter is a weapon designed to penetrate certain types of containers and shatter components and circuitry before the detonator can be initiated. The shotgun is good for smashing up components and chopping wires.

We set the Wheelbarrow on its way between the right-hand pair of rails, eyeballing its direction of travel. The No. 2 flicks the switch on the control box that stops the left track for a second and allows the machine to straighten up. Then, because he's over-compensated, it's a sharp flick on the right switch. Then it's both tracks forward and away it goes, up and over, up and over each concrete sleeper until it's in the vicinity of the target. Then it's all eyes to the CCTV monitor. He brings the RCV up close to the main target: the TPU. Then, by extending the boom over the track, he brings the Disrupter up close to the TPU, inching forward until the Disrupter is almost touching it. Then it stops. I say, 'OK, let's do it.'

A warning is passed to all troops to expect a controlled explosion. It's fingers in the ears time in case it doesn't quite go according to plan and all eyes are on the CCTV monitor. Then, 'Boom!' The sound is akin to a shotgun blast and the TPU disintegrates. It's overkill frankly, but I don't have a smaller weapon in the armoury that is as reliable. We use the Wheelbarrow to roll the keg around a bit and up-end it. This movement doesn't eliminate everything; I still need to see inside the keg. The only quick and safe way of doing this is to cut the keg in half. Gone are the days when a hacksaw might

Controlled explosion on the firing mechanism. Wheelbarrow at its best.

have had to be considered. Today, we have a specialist explosive weapon called Flatsword. It's a hardened metal blade contained in a large wooden cassette. It's cumbersome and heavy, and the blade is projected by a kilogram of military high explosive. The weapon isn't something we're encouraged to use in built-up areas or back on the UK mainland even, but here in the open there's little chance of collateral damage. Because of the rough terrain, the cassette would fall apart if we tried to deliver it using the RCV, so I have to carry it to the device myself.

The weapon is fitted into its frame and primed with the sheet explosives. An electric detonator is connected to a twin flex cable and inserted into the plastic receptor. Lifting the weapon and pointing it forward, I begin the perilous journey to the target. It's perilous mainly because, with the weight of the cassette, the uneven ground and the clumsy suit, I'm likely to stumble and break my bloody leg before I even get to the target. Safety conscious as I am, though, I have the weapon facing forward and the satisfaction of knowing that if the weapon should function prematurely I will not be cut in half. The IEDD suit would in this case be helpful, but only in reducing the effort of those who would have to recover me, since what would remain would be big pieces.

My heavy breathing soon steams up the visor. I can only vaguely make out the beer keg in the middle distance and I can't see anything immediately in front of me. Then, within 20 ft of the keg, I'm yanked to a halt. It's fortunate that my end of the cable is tied to the metal frame; otherwise, the force would have ripped out the detonator. The electrical twin flex cable is being fed out from a reel back at the control point. I curse and turn back to see what's going on. Frantic efforts are being made to sort it out. The cable, as it is apt to do if one takes one's eyes off it, has unravelled too quickly and tangled itself around the reel. But, whilst they wrestle with the problem, I'm left standing a few feet short of the device and well within the danger area. I place the weapon on the ground and push up the visor to shout at the team. 'Lift up the reel and come forward with it.' One of the guys signals that he's understood and I turn back to the job in hand. I don't bother to pull the visor down this time. As the No. 2 carries the reel forward with its tangled cable, I haul the weapon the last few feet to the target. I position the stand so that the forward part of the cassette is within a few inches of the beer keg. I don't have to mess about with the height as we have it set about right.

Back at the control point now, the electronic firing switch is connected to the unjammed firing cable and primed by the No. 2. I give a warning to the ground troops and for everyone local to get under cover. Then, on the shout, 'Firing!' the buttons are pressed and 'Bang!'

The controlled explosion is much more substantial this time. As the smoke dissipates we can see that the metal container has been cut neatly in two. The bottom half looks as if it hasn't moved.

I give it a minute or so and then walk back up to it. Two types of home-made explosives are spread about. Together they weigh about 60 lb. Nothing else of a sinister nature is evident. We bag up the forensics, clear down and move out. The railway is unscathed and will quickly get back to normal.

Had the device functioned, it would have produced a bloody great hole in the ground, taking out all four rails and possibly the adjacent bridge. All this would have completely messed up the BR timetable for a week or so at least.

Looking about me as the lads pack up, I'm conscious that it's only when we finish and leave the area that the infantry can follow. I may be here to support them, but they're fundamental to my team's security. If I take two or three days over a job, which can happen, then it's the infantry who have to stay out in the freezing fields to maintain the cordon. I decide that, within reason, I'll try and speed up my side of any clearance operations – with 'within reason' underlined. The alternative is to pay slavish attention to our Render Safe Procedures. Although they err on the side of safety, and we have them for a very good reason; they can massively increase the time taken to complete an operation. Applying our procedures pedantically, just as they are written, without too much thought, takes you into the realm of the trained monkey. The RSPs will get you there, but not anytime soon. Sometimes, however, the threat can be over-egged and an operator can be too cautious. Like many things in life there is a balance to be found. This is no different in that respect.

26th January 1981

Explosion, Golden Griddle Restaurant, Newry

In the intervening period, I'm called to deal with two minor incidents. One is the discovery of an army rifle grenade, which was reported lost by a foot patrol a long time ago. Lost equipment when found is a real headache, because you can never be sure it hasn't been tampered with. I destroy it in a controlled explosion.

The second is an army torch, also lost and now found and feared to be booby trapped. I X-ray it. It isn't.

On 26th January, I'm tasked to an incident in Newry. At 6 p.m. three women are present in the Golden Griddle restaurant in Sandy Street when two armed men, shouting 'IRA', enter it and place a blue holdall next to the counter. The bomb hasn't gone off yet and, as we can deploy by vehicle, there's a lot of urgency. Using the wall map we pinpoint the street and quickly decide on a route in. Now we're moving as fast as possible. Everyone knows the drill; no orders need to be given. The adrenalin flows as I jog down the corridor towards the courtyard. At the same time, I'm fastening my flack jacket and the chin strap on my crash helmet. A crash-out like this may be the norm for teams in Belfast or Londonderry, but for us it's the exception.

'Good luck, Felix,' I hear someone say.

The Transit is already moving by the time I get to it. Hauling open the door, I leap into the front seat and inadvertently crash the clumsy helmet against the door jamb. I curse. The blue lights are on as we roar out of the Mill past the entrance sangar. I don't see any of it because my head is down logging the incident in my note book. I don't feel fear, only excitement.

I reckon we're about halfway there when the radio bursts into life and Bessbrook Ops speak to us. 'Hello 45 Echo, this is Zero. Rucksack at the scene have reported that the device has functioned. Over.'

'Bollocks!' I shout before responding in my best radio voice. '45 Echo. OK, thanks, we'll be at the task location in about 10 minutes. Out.'

It's an anticlimax; we're all disappointed. I feel the adrenalin and the excitement subsiding. At the scene, the RUC are with the owner of the restaurant – one of the ladies present when the bombers burst in. The restaurant hasn't caught fire. I listen to her story and then have a look inside. The restaurant is a mess consistent with about 4–5 kg of HME. I declare the area clear. Understandably, the lady is upset, but she tries to hide it. I find parts of a CO_2 gas cylinder, which substantiates my estimation. The only real casualty is the owner's cat whose curiosity has sadly been its undoing.

27th January 1981

Explosion, Railway Line, Meigh

At 9 p.m. I'm notified that the main Belfast to Dundalk railway line has been attacked again. I'm also notified that the Killeavy Truck Company, a vehicle yard adjacent to the railway, has been destroyed by fire and explosion. Both attacks have obviously been carried out by the same PIRA unit. It's their way of making up for the failed beer keg attack four days earlier. I guess we're dealing with people who take things very personally.

We deploy the next day to the railway line and I get on the ground late at about 2 p.m. I find that one rail is very severely bent and twisted. Under this is a relatively small crater: the seat of the explosion. The damage is consistent with about 2–3 kg of commercial explosive. I declare the area clear. This is always a risky call, because you can only really declare something safe that you can see and evaluate. The fact that nothing else is found doesn't always mean something isn't there, lurking, poised to catch you out. There's only so much that can be searched.

It's too late to begin the vehicle yard investigation, so the job is postponed until tomorrow. As light fades we're extracted by helicopter back to Bessbrook.

28th January 1981

Blast Incendiary, Killeavy Truck Company

Trucks burnt out, cabs and dash boards melted like giant candles.
It must have been a regular fireworks display.

The next day we're back on the scene. I decide not to bring the Wheelbarrow as I think we're only investigating a series of explosions. The Wheelbarrow would have to be transported on one of our two heli-portable vehicles and moving all this around the countryside via helicopter is a bit of a logistics exercise.

The large metal gates at the entrance of the truck company are wide open. It's a big yard full of machinery, large trucks and tankers. Everything has cooled down nicely and there's no sign of the fires that must have raged two nights before. Just about all the equipment and trucks are burnt out: an insurance write-off. Truck cabs are melted like large wax candles. I can see some lightweight buildings, which I assume are the offices and workshops. They appear unscathed.

I set up our control point just outside the entrance. The Royal Engineer Searchers do their job and sweep through the whole area, reporting the seats of many explosions as they go. Then I get news that one of the searchers has discovered an unexploded device in the cab of a large truck. He describes it as a 1-gallon Jeyes fluid can, which has a metal-cased explosive charge taped to it. On the cab floor, adjacent to the can, is a plywood TPU. The device is a blast incendiary. A gallon of petrol detonated in this way is quite spectacular. All of a sudden the job takes on a wholly different complexion.

I contemplate the IEDD suit. It's heavy, comprised as it is of very many laminated nylon sheets. It does have its uses; for example, it will save me from the blast should the small cased charge detonate. It will also reduce the effects of exploding petrol. Most importantly, it will keep me warm as it's bloody freezing. Better on than off then!

I step into the trousers first. These are held up by cotton tape braces, which are tied in a bow across my chest. The backs of the leg are zipped up. I put my hands into the heavy jacket with its thick collar and this is again zipped up at the rear. Two large Makrolon armoured plates are inserted into pockets in the front of the jacket. There are gloves, but no one wears them because of the loss of dexterity. The helmet is very heavy with its thick plastic visor, so I elect instead to wear a lightweight, visored crash helmet, which is much less cumbersome and doesn't steam up quite as quickly. The suit manufacturers will say that wearing a lightweight helmet completely negates the effectiveness of the suit. I'm sure they're right, but I'll take my chances.

Taking a Disrupter, a hook and line, and also the Pentax 35mm camera, I approach the device. I don't see that I'm up against the clock here as the time will have long expired on the type of clockwork timer PIRA uses. Of course there is always the chance that you are being confronted by a new innovation or a new technology. This is what makes the work unpredictable.

The door of the vehicle is open and, peering around it, I see that the device stands on the cab floor in the passenger well. It's at my head height. Everything about the device is as described except for one other thing, which is odd – the dowel pin, by which the device is normally armed, is still in place. Odd things are always highly suspicious and I'm a lot less comfortable now than I was five minutes ago.

The blast incendiary - a device with an odd secret.

Does it mean the device is safe, i.e. unarmed? Well, it would be madness to assume it is. There is every possibility that the can, in fact, contains a separate device with an anti-lift switch incorporated. If so, the device will function when it's moved a few millimetres. PIRA have used this type of booby trap in the past with tragic consequences for one of our operators. I take a photograph of the device and then get on with the job.

Ideally, I'd destroy the TPU with the Disrupter and take out the can at the same time. Unfortunately, there's insufficient room to position the long metal tube without a risk of disturbing the device. Where is the Wheelbarrow when I need it? I elect instead to 'hoik' the device out to somewhere I can get at it and for this I'll use the ubiquitous 'hook and line'. This may seem to be a passive way of dealing with it, but we need to get the job done and get out. I'm conscious that an awful lot of soldiers are tied up in an operation protecting a pile of burned-out trucks.

I take a deep breath and very gingerly place the line around the device and then back off.

Back at the control point and breathing again, I gently take up the slack in the rope. Pulling on the rope I hear the device hit the ground with a dull clunk. This tells me the can is full of something or other. The device might have gone off at that point, but has chosen not to. I leave it for a short period, a 'secondary soak', as we say, before approaching it once again with the Disrupter. But I don't need it. The components are spread over the ground. If you can't always be careful in this job at the very least you need to be lucky.

The lid of the TPU has detached itself and the entire electrical circuit is visible. Examining it, I can see that the TPU has, in fact, been rewired. The clothes peg arming switch is no longer in the firing circuit. This means that the device was always armed despite the dowel pin and should have functioned when the timer ran out. It will be for the forensic science lab to determine why the device failed to function.

Separating out the components with a pair of wire cutters.

Petrol is leaking out of the can. I check the base of it for anything untoward: it's clear. Using a Stanley knife, I cut the tape that secures the cased charge to the can and then, with a pair of wire cutters, I separate the cased charge from the TPU and tape up the ends of each wire. The device is effectively neutralised now. I take the bits back to the control point and we bag them up – all except the cased charge. This could be unstable and, therefore, isn't transportable. For evidential purposes, I take an X-ray of its inner workings with my portable X-ray equipment and then destroy it in a small controlled explosion.

As was touched on earlier, at the beginning of the NI Campaign, the X-ray equipment was considered very much a prime bit of kit. The RSP then would be to X-ray the object in order to confirm it was a device before tackling it. Today, the facility is still used, but primarily to confirm the contents of an

object once any associated hazards have been dealt with. The equipment I have with me now is like an elongated squared-off torch that I can carry with one hand. We also use Polaroid film, thus dispensing with tins of developer and fixer. These days it's all nice and tidy.

Whilst the lads pack up, I go on to examine the remainder of the yard. A mixture of blast incendiaries and gas cylinder-type devices have indeed been used: a total of ten in all. It must have been quite a fireworks display. The fragments of gas cylinders and metal cans are collected and bagged up for forensics – job done – and it's back to Bessbrook.

Left: Recovering the remains of the devices for the forensic lab.

Below: Checking out the rest of the damage.

However, this task doesn't actually end here; there's a postscript. At 9 p.m. that evening I'm called to a discussion at the ops room. A torch has subsequently been discovered on a tanker at the vehicle yard. No one admits to owning it and so it will have to be cleared. The problem is that, because the area is well within 'bandit country', a second fully fledged clearance operation will have to be mounted. No one wants that. A plan is therefore devised that would get the job done with the minimum number of troops.

The Close Observation Platoon (COP) is a group of soldiers who carry out specialist covert and surveillance operations. They are going to form a protection party for me and my No. 2. We'll use two civilian (i.e. covert) cars, so it's civilian clothes. My No. 2 and I will be in the first car with two armed escorts. We'll travel in convoy through deepest South Armagh to arrive at the end of the lane where the vehicle yard is located. Our car will then drive forward to the yard and my No. 2 and I will leap out with our IEDD equipment. The car will then drive on to the other end of the lane and the soldiers will cordon and secure it. The soldiers in the other car will already have secured the other end of the lane. We expect to be in and out of there in fifteen minutes. It all sounds simple, but that is the way of it with plans.

Our car screeches to a halt. The two of us leap out with our hands full of equipment. The car roars off into the darkness. It's silent. It's also pitch black; I can't see a bloody thing. I run to where I think the yard is, straight into the gate. Crash! I have a gate imprinted on my face. 'Shit, we're locked out!' I whisper.

As my eyes become accustomed to the darkness, I see that the owners have rebuilt the perimeter fence and closed and padlocked the large gates for good measure. We don't have a radio to tell anyone this, so, by the time our vehicle comes to collect us, we're still trying to get over the fence.

'Have you finished?' hisses the voice of impatience from somewhere behind and below me.

'I haven't f*cking started,' I hiss back. 'Can you give us a bloody hand?'

He dumps his ArmaLite and gets stuck in. I swear it's like a Laurel and Hardy movie. You couldn't make it up.

Looking into the yard from the top of the fence, I can see that if I do eventually get in I probably won't be able to get out again. Brilliant! Also nagging at me is the thought that this is the stamping ground of some really nasty bad guys. Them turning up isn't completely in the realms of fantasy. If they do, I think, there is every possibility they will laugh themselves to death!

I finally get over the fence using the gate pillar and eventually locate the torch, which is on the horizontal ladder along the top of a tanker. It's an army torch. One of the search team members has probably left it behind – maybe.

I can't easily position the X-ray equipment, so I elect instead to tumble the torch off the tanker with the hook and line. Down it comes with a thump. I lift it. The weight is spot on. I take a chance and open it up from the front, removing the bulb and reflector. It's clear.

After another ten minutes scrambling back up the fence with half the COP helping, we're out of there.

It wasn't the most well-executed operation or RSP I'd ever been party to, but it had to have been one of the funniest!

30th January 1981

Derrybeg Community Centre – A Riotous Assembly

Over the next couple of days, I deal with two more incidents in Newry. One is the routine clearance of a stolen car spotted in a housing estate. The other involves two suspicious devices discovered at the Derrybeg Community Centre. With regards to the latter, it's late evening when they're reported and troops are reluctant to go into this housing estate at night in case it's a trap – a 'come on' situation. The job is, therefore, left until next day.

Next morning we're at the scene and I quickly come to accept the army view of the estate. Whilst I'm working to clear the devices, soldiers on the outer cordon find themselves having to contain a small riot. This isn't anticipated, so the troops don't have the proper gear to defend themselves. A car is set on fire and there's a lot of shouting and stick waving. The cordon doesn't look especially secure and is never too far from collapsing. I keep one eye on all that is happening behind me since I'm obliged to abandon the task if my team's protection can't be guaranteed. Neither I nor the team are trained in riot drills, so if anyone nasty does get too close they're likely to get much more than they bargained for. Anybody who has seen close up, or has been involved in a riot will testify that behaviour can quickly transmogrify into the grotesque and lead to unforeseen and tragic consequences, especially if the situation is underestimated and control is lost. These thoughts incentivise me into not hanging about. Two items in our IEDD equipment schedule are semi-automatic shotguns – one of which is sawn-off. I keep the latter close to hand, having concluded that if push comes to shove, and I have to invite someone to make my day, it will be a much more useful deterrent than my 9mm Browning pistol.

In a short time, cutting one or two corners, I discover that both devices are hoaxes. I conclude that they have, in all likelihood, been planted by the youths outside who wished to get troops into the area for some sport. Thankfully, everyone gets out in one piece and the Derrybeg Community Centre is left unscathed.

3rd February 1981

Ambush Device, Chancellors Road, Bessbrook

Three days later at 3.20 p.m. the wall-mounted plastic intercom by my bed bursts in to life. 'Can you come through to the ops room, Felix?' It's more of a command than a question.

'Certainly, sir,' says I. Such calls generally mean business.

A group of people await my arrival. The duty ops officer is accompanied by two policemen and a civilian.

'Felix,' says the ops officer, 'this is Mr X. He works for the council. Earlier today, while clearing debris from culverts on the Chancellors Road, he came across a number of milk churns in one of them.'

I speak with the guy. He thinks there are three churns. There isn't much else he can tell me as he didn't hang around!

The senior police officer takes me to one side and continues. 'This coincides with three telephone calls we've received over the last 10 days stating that a farm was on fire in that area. On each occasion a covert police car responded but no fire was found. We considered the calls hoaxes.'

It didn't need a brain surgeon to work out that PIRA had tried to entice the police into the area with the intention of detonating the device as their car passed over it. It hadn't happened only because the bomber had been unable to identify the police vehicle. Fortunately, no military vehicle had used that road recently. The road is now out of bounds to all security forces.

A helicopter is called up and we reconnoitre the area. I'm accompanied by a company commander who will be in overall charge of the operation and also the Royal Engineers Search Adviser. All of us need to see the lie of the land for our differing purposes.

CULVERTS

Ireland is green and wet because an awful lot of weather comes in off the Atlantic. It is also a terrain of undulating hills and lakes and is therefore criss-crossed by a great many streams. Wherever a stream comes up against a road, a tunnel has to be constructed to allow the stream through. There are thousands of these. PIRA realised early on that culverts are ideal for concealing large ambush bombs and many members of the Security Forces have come to grief from this form of attack.

The helicopter circles the culvert and I peer down. There's a stone parapet directly opposite a white gated driveway. I can see the culvert entrance, which is about 4 ft high. It's quite well concealed from the road as it's surrounded by hedges. It's not so easy, though, to see the stream's route up to where it runs into the culvert. I also take this opportunity to look for an area that will make a suitable control point – not too close, not too far away. And because of what I will have to do, I need a straight run at it.

The next day, at first light, the infantry move into the area and dig in. The surrounding high ground is dominated; the roads are sealed off; traffic is diverted and a cordon is put in place.

Once the area is declared secure, the Royal Engineer Search team of the Parachute Regiment go in. Using their electronic detection equipment and sniffer dogs, they sweep the hedges and road for any additional devices. They also search our landing site. This work can be very risky since a searcher won't detect a device until they are pretty much upon it.

All the equipment I require is packed onto 'Gobbler'. Who gave it this

A culvert with a deadly secret.

code name I do not know. It's a Land Rover, but you wouldn't recognise it as such. It's stripped down to the very basics to make it heli-portable. The Wheelbarrow stays behind again. Despite having tracks, it doesn't work particularly well on rough ground. In any case, this job is going to require a number of manual approaches.

I've selected a landing site about 400 metres from the culvert and this is where the helicopters deposit us. We leap out and release the under-slung vehicle from the second chopper. The din from the helicopter engines is deafening, it's impossible to speak and hand signals are the order of the day. It's a relief when they finally lift off and roar away into the grey sky. Silence and tranquillity descend again on another wet, muddy field. At least it's not raining. Anybody else might think the area is picturesque, but, for now, it's too cold to even notice it and there is far too much to do.

I look around me at the hedges and ground. It's a nervous time because even at this early juncture we're trying to outthink the terrorist. If they've second-guessed our landing site we could already be in trouble.

Because our ropes and cables are only so long, we need to be much nearer to the target. We move forward to the agreed control point about 80 metres from the culvert. We're perilously close if the device should function for there's an awful lot of heavy stuff to be flung into the air and precious little cover.

The RE Search Adviser (RESA), a staff sergeant, approaches me. His men have discovered the twin flex command wire that was to have detonated the device. It's been laid above ground and enters the culvert from the far side.

A safety procedure is that I chop the command wire before making an approach to the culvert, thus isolating the terrorist firing point from the device. I take the red explosives box, a firing cable and some other equipment and, with my No. 2, follow the search adviser down to the road, giving the culvert a wide berth.

No real attempt has been made to conceal the cable and it follows a line of hedgerows towards the top of the ridge line about 300 metres from the culvert.

Everything we do in IEDD, we try to do remotely. This is no exception. Attaching a small explosive charge to the twin flex, I run out a firing cable and then fire it. The bang echoes all around the hills. If the locals didn't know we were here before, they do now. I test the electrical circuit in both directions. There's a circuit at the culvert end which tells me that a detonator is connected and the device is primed. The circuit is open at the other end. If I'd found this to be the other way around, then the job would have become even more interesting. That is on the basis that you don't really want to live in interesting times.

The search teams have now located the terrorist firing point and report that a large blue battery pack is lying in the grass there. I'll deal with that later; the culvert is the priority.

We get back to the control point across the other side of the road and make the final arrangements. In particular, the Electronic Counter Measures equipment is switched on and warmed up. The RF output will provide me with an electronic safety umbrella against the current range of radio controlled devices. At least that's what we're taught. Everything is now set and I can't put off the inevitable any longer.

I grasp the end of our car tow rope. It's strong and it needs to be; one milk churn full of home-made explosives will weigh at least 100 lb (50 kilos) and I'm going to use this rope to drag the churns out of the culvert. I put the 35 mm Pentax camera in my pocket along with a pair of wire cutters and a Stanley knife. I also take with me a primed Disrupter in case I come across something unexpected that I could use it on. I don't wear the IEDD suit as it's far too cumbersome and, in any case, won't be much use if anything goes wrong. Then I'm on my way. Someone says good luck. Team members play out the cables from the reels and I take that lonely path up to the culvert entrance. At this point I have to believe we've done everything we can to reduce the risks in my favour, but you never really know what you're dealing with until afterwards. For example, the milk churns might even be a decoy and I'm approaching the culvert exactly how the terrorist might have assumed I would. It's a nervy time.

Arriving at the entrance, I look around for anything out of the ordinary: wires, disturbed earth, etc. I feel my heart thumping. I'm not cold any more. I take a deep breath and drop down off the concrete retaining wall into the shallow stream with a splash. The only noise now is my laboured breathing and the seemingly magnified twittering of a bird somewhere nearby. I look into the culvert. It's fairly gloomy, but, as my eyes accustom to it, I can see there are far more than the three milk churns I was told about. I count six, maybe seven.

A quarter of a ton of explosives in seven milk churns.

There is probably a quarter of a ton of high explosives. I'm not overly alarmed because, from where I'm standing, it doesn't make much difference.

I set the camera shutter to a low speed, so the flash doesn't go off when I use it, and take a photograph. If it doesn't work out, there may at least be a record of what it looked like for others to mull over. I don't dwell on the reality, which is that, if the device does function, the crater would be massive and the camera would probably be dust – like me.

Leaving both the camera and Disrupter behind on the grass bank and with a sense of dread, I crawl up the cold stone tunnel on all fours, dragging the tow rope behind me. The water's not deep, but my legs are quickly soaked up to the knees. I bang my head on a horizontal metal girder and swear. From here on in, I swear to myself a lot – all the way in and pretty much all the way out. It's a bit like talking oneself up.

It must have been quite a feat lifting these heavy churns into place. It will have been dark and I can imagine the fevered activity and their nervousness, never quite sure if the Security Forces are going to turn up unannounced and slot them. Shame that, because if they had, it would have saved me all this sweat.

The silver grey churns stand close together, linked with white det cord. Altogether, there's six full-size churns and a half-size creamery can. Inside each churn will be the main HME charge and a booster charge. I look for electric detonator leads, but can't see them. Logically, it's going to be on the far side since that's where the command wire enters the tunnel.

The whole thing is so big I can't easily get around it. Squeezing past and possibly disturbing a churn isn't a viable option for obvious reasons. My breath is rapid, shallow now. I feel light-headed and I'm still cursing. I'd like to say my

THE DRAGON

Cloying black and wet the night, I spend it contemplating
the creature with a wicked heart that 'neath the lane lies waiting.

We have it planned. I've talked the talk. There's nothing left to do
'cept now it's time to walk the walk that he or I must lose.

See the culvert and the tunnel, step, step, step to the dragon's lair
Sanity strained and senses funnelled, shivers in the Armagh air.

Feel the east wind it is all knowing, guess the soul that I had time to bear
as gently I ease into the stream a'flowing, visible now to its steely stare.

The hydra heads are bunched up tight, their caps and voices sealed
with bile and energy packed inside, what mischief might be revealed.

Around its guts the water frets, I hear its manic scrabbling
pushing against the alloy vests, and sweeping by still babbling.

Feeling colder, inching still closer, the stalactites drip, dripping, drop.
They tap, tap, tap on the dragons shoulder, like a tick, tick, ticking, clock.

A necklace links it all together, suspended, that white crack of doom,
with beating heart that seems forever, I reach out into the fetid gloom.

I gave it my all, for I'd made my peace at the end of that sleepless night.
I promised that I would slay the beast or die in the early light.

mind is crystal clear but it isn't. My senses are straining for anything out of the ordinary. Outside, everyone is behind cover, nervously anticipating the outcome of my approach, waiting, probably wondering what the bloody hell I'm doing that's taking so long. How many minutes have actually passed since I entered the tunnel, I do not know. But it feels as if I've taken too long.

I abandon an attempt at getting to the detonator. Instead, I get on with what I primarily set out to do. I thread the thick rope through the handles of two milk churns. Extracting two churns at a time will reduce the number of approaches I have to make. I don't cut the det cord because I can't be absolutely sure that it is det cord.

I make my way out of the tunnel and climb back up the bank. Then I walk fairly casually back to the control point, but watching the ground extremely carefully (this time to avoid stepping into a cow pat). Back at the control point,

I pass the revised estimate of the device size to the Incident Commander and HQ Bessbrook.

Using our vehicle's four wheel drive capability, we drag the first two churns out into the light of day. It's a bit of a battle. The vehicle skids around and the tow rope stretches alarmingly, such that, if it snapped, it would probably take someone's head off. It doesn't, so the extraction is fairly uneventful.

In all, I have to make four approaches into the culvert. As they are extracted I line the churns up against the thick concrete retaining wall ready for the next phase.

Someone taps me on the shoulder. 'We're being watched,' he says, and points to a rise some 200 metres behind us. Sure enough, I can see a face peering through a hedge. Without camouflage cream, his bare skin almost glows in the dark hedge. This is quite disconcerting and everything comes to a grinding halt immediately. I notify the incident commander and we take cover.

Something similar to this occurred in the Cortreasla Bridge incident six years ago, which wiped out the Bessbrook team,. A man was seen then, but no action was taken. We've learned from that.

The radio traffic hots up and in short time the throbbing vibration of a helicopter engine is heard. It rears up into view over a hedge and skids to a halt in an adjacent field. As we watch, soldiers pour out of the machine and the guy is apprehended and bundled away.

We get back to work. Sometime later, we're informed that the face is a local farmhand whose curiosity had apparently got the better of him. Well fine, but I remain sceptical. The people who detonate these devices are just like him. They're local, know the area and appear very normal when you see them in court. In his case, his curiosity could easily have got him killed because, if something untoward had occurred at the time he was spotted, he would have taken the can for it. Soldiers are, for a number of historical reasons, very twitchy during these operations.

I recover the electric detonator still attached to a piece of det cord. A made-up test circuit and bulb is also found, which the bomber has used to test the electrical continuity of the device, but then, as if by magic, it is lost in the post-clearance activities, never to be seen again.

Rolls of coloured insulation tape are also recovered, which the bomber has used to connect up all the bomb components. The rolls have been abandoned by the terrorist because a court of law has undoubtedly educated them in the folly of retaining them.

The device is neutralised now, but isn't completely rendered safe. Each churn could contain a secondary switch of some sort. Three ATOs have already died having underestimated the lethal potential of milk churns. The clearance continues,

50% of the way through the Operation. The churns have been extracted from the culvert; neutralised but yet to be rendered safe.

Most of the churns are cut in half, the others up-ended to spill out the contents.

therefore. Over the next hour or so, I'm backward and forward setting and firing specialised cutting charges and, when we run out of the charges, I up-end the remaining churns with ropes and shake out the contents. At the end of this exercise everything is spread about and visible and so I'm able to declare the thing safe.

Two types of home-made explosives have been used and I take 30g samples of each for forensic evidence. As the explosives are fertiliser-based, the bulk of it is spread out on the fields. This is standard procedure because they're quickly desensitised by moisture and soon absorbed into the ground. The second explosive type is the booster charge and this contains a chemical called nitrobenzene. NB has a very strong smell of marzipan. To try and contain this distinctive stink it is often wrapped in layers of polythene. NB is a compound that contaminates everything it comes into contact with. I wear plastic gloves when handling it because it's corrosive, carcinogenic and easily absorbed through the pores of the skin. These attributes may or may not be understood by PIRA. If not, then a lot of their operatives can expect to have serious health problems in due course. I dissolve this explosive in copious amounts of water before spreading it out on the field in the same way.

With the area made safe, we clear down and pack up. I still have the terrorist firing point to think about, but, with light fading fast, it's a job for tomorrow. I ask the troops to call in the chopper and we're extracted back to Bessbrook HQ. Not the infantry though; on this occasion they stay out on the ground to keep the area secure.

There's a good reason why we're extracted back to Bessbrook each evening. It's not, as is often unkindly suggested, because we aren't sufficiently hardy to withstand a night out on the freezing hills, but because we need to be on standby in the event of an emergency in Newry – or elsewhere for that matter. At least that's what I tell everybody.

5th February 1981

Booby Trap, Chancellors Road, Bessbrook

The next day at first light, I'm on the ground again. We set up the control point along the ridge line, about 100 metres from the terrorist firing point.

Wearing the IEDD suit this time, and with both a Disrupter and hook and line, I make my way to the terrorist firing point. I step warily. The Royal Engineer Searchers have done their bit, but the immediate area of the target is my concern. It's common for a pressure plate-type device to be laid in these circumstances. On this occasion, I'm very happy to find that the whole area has been recently trampled by cows.

Arriving at the firing point, the first thing I see is the bright blue tape of the battery pack lying exposed alongside the long wet grass and hedge. It comprises

The Parachute Regiment Search team is at work. The position of the firing cable has been drawn into the picture.

a set of large 9-volt batteries strapped together with blue adhesive tape. Looking to my left I see a gap in the hedge from where the terrorist bomber will have watched the traffic at the bottom of the hill. The culvert can be clearly seen. It's an ideal vantage point, which must have been well reconnoitred by them beforehand. I can imagine the bomber, CB radio in hand, nervously awaiting the tip-off from his compatriot parked at the entrance to the lane that the police car was on its way.

I lean forward to position the Disrupter and then catch my breath. I see a taut fishing line – very thin but unmistakable. It's attached to the battery pack. I lean forward. The other end disappears into the undergrowth.

Stepping to one side, I carefully part the undergrowth and there, wrapped in a fertiliser sack, is a cast-iron gas cylinder which if full contains about 10lb HME. I take the whole thing in, in a second. The nylon fishing line is attached to the dowel pin of a plywood TPU. On this occasion, it's providing the firing switch to the device via a pair of red and yellow electric detonator leads. The detonator is attached to a length of det cord protruding from the top of the cylinder.

I've seen enough and depart the scene to gather my thoughts.

Having talked it through with the team, I return to the device some time later. Attaching a hook and line to the plastic sack, I pull the whole thing out of the undergrowth. Approaching it again, I remove the detonator from the det cord and disconnect the leads from the TPU. The whole thing is recovered intact.

The Victim Operated Device components with the Command Wire cable reel.

The battery pack gets X-rayed for good measure and the guts of it are found to be clear. We don't have equipment for opening up something as heavy duty as a cast-iron cylinder and unscrewing the metal bung is too risky. Therefore, submitting it to the forensic science laboratory is also too risky. I destroy it in a controlled explosion using 8 oz of plastic explosives. Job done. Everything has gone pretty well – or so I think.

As we're packing up, the SATO arrives. It's the first time I've seen him since our inaugural meeting. I'm polite and I try to relax, but we're both ill at ease. He doesn't say anything to ease the situation and there are no words of praise for the team. The culvert device yesterday doesn't even get a mention. I wonder if he's actually disappointed. He sets to, fiddling with the forensic evidence, and then the conversation is all about how I could have tackled the job differently. Normally, I'd be happy to walk through the disposal approach, but coming from him I'm unsure if it's legitimate criticism or pique, because I've achieved something useful. It might sound unprofessional but, unfortunately, that is how it was.

I don't argue with him. He has his say and leaves. Everyone else is elated though. It's been a great team effort and the infantry unit is well pleased. The CATO telephones me that evening and he's quite effusive. The photograph of the culvert device is displayed at the British Army Headquarters in Lisburn all the following week.

The PIRA planners have failed again and we can surmise that they're unlikely to let it ride. We hear a rumour that they are desperate for a success in our area. I guess their credibility depends on it; at least that's how they probably see it.

VIP Visits

Periodically VIPs visit the Mill and I brief them on our work and also demonstrate Wheelbarrow. If we like them, they get to play with it.

Anyone with an eye for detail will see in the top photograph that I have shielded this MP from a highly offensive but amusing poster that will get me into

Left: Discussing our role with a Member of Parliament.

Right: The QLR Adjutant looks on as the MP demonstrates his prowess with our Wheelbarrow.

bother downstream. I am also showing off the latest technology for producing my IEDD Reports. And anyone with an eye for style will note that moustaches are de rigueur for soldiers wishing to exhibit that little *je ne sais quoi!*

12TH FEBRUARY 1981

Ambush Devices, Border Crossing H25A

Eight months previously, on 14th June 1980, the Southern Irish Police, the Garda, discovered a twin flex command wire on their side of the border, near to the crossing we call H25A. The border at that place is delineated by a small stream and is not far from Crossmaglen.

The Garda cut the wire and threw the loose end into the North. From December 1980, a number of explosions have been heard in this area and on 25th January 1981 a farm owner reports damage to his adjacent outbuildings. A second command wire is then discovered by the Garda due south of the farm complex.

From our point of view, this area stinks and is, therefore, left to stew (or 'soak' as we tend to call it). The enemy is always trying to lure soldiers into a trap. They're very good at it, but, over the years, we have also got a lot better at seeing through them.

The infantry regiment decides to combine both clearances into one operation and on 18th February 1981 we go in. The command wire south of the farm is dealt with first. The Royal Engineers trace its whole length and measure it at 500 metres long. It's buried to a depth of 6–8 inches and has been in position for at least a number of years. It's a pig to remove and, in the end, we content ourselves with snapping it in lots of places and reburying the breaks, thereby rendering it unusable. The wire leads to a tight bend in a country lane. No device is discovered attached to it and so we move on to our next arranged control point to investigate the explosions and the second command wire.

This command wire straddles the border. It's been fed through a plastic hosepipe, which is held in place on the bed of the stream by rocks. On our side, it's well buried and difficult to trace, but it points towards some dry stone walls that circle high ground overlooking the farm buildings, about 150 metres from the border. Displacing a couple of stones in the wall reveals a plastic fertiliser sack and inside is a stainless steel gas cylinder, which I estimate to contains about 30 lb of HME. A twig with an electrical detonator taped to it has been pushed into the explosives. The detonator is seriously corroded, having been in contact with the HME for quite some time. Corrosion can make detonators extremely sensitive. I remove it carefully. Using a hook and line, the

Crossing H25A

Explosions x2

IED 2

IED 1

The Command Wire and position of the IED's have been drawn into the picture.

Above: The first device hidden in the dry stone wall at the end of the Command Wire.

Right: The second device was wired to a junction in the Command Wire and designed to function simultaneously with the other.

device is pulled out of its hiding place into the open and we go on to recover the remainder of the command wire. It's whilst we're reeling in the cable that a taped junction is spotted in the wire about 10ft from the device. This reveals a second twin flex cable. Stopping everything, everyone is evacuated from the immediate area to a place of safety again. I come back and trace the twin flex cable to an adjacent wall just a few feet away from the first. Sure enough, after tumbling the wall with a hook and line, I find a second gas cylinder hidden in the wall, which is also wrapped in heavy plastic sheeting. This also has a corroded detonator pushed into the explosives, which I carefully withdraw.

Whilst there's no firing mechanism to speak of, the danger is from the HME itself, which has been mixed for some time and is potentially unstable. It could spontaneously combust and this would create either a low-order explosion or even burn to a high-order detonation. Either way, it would be a shame to get myself killed at this late stage in the proceedings.

Bringing water from the stream, I do what I can to desensitise the explosives. Then I carry the cylinders into a field and destroy both in separate controlled explosions.

We go on to investigate the derelict buildings. These have been destroyed by two relatively small explosions. All in all, it has taken two days to complete the operation.

The conclusions I draw are that the first command wire, laid some years previously, was to have been used in an attack on a Security Force patrol. The device would have been concealed behind the dry stone wall at a bend in the road where any vehicle would have had to slow down. Because green vehicle movements are banned now in this area, the wire was, to most intents and purposes, redundant.

The explosions in the derelicts are completely separate. These were staged to entice SF into the area in order to utilise the two devices well concealed in the dry stone walls. Rusty food tins (i.e. army 'compo') are evidence that troops had, at sometime in the not-too-distant past, used the high ground as an observation post. Littering the countryside like this might eventually damage your mate's health!

24TH FEBRUARY 1981

Car Clearance, Vicinity Omeath Road

Just over two months have passed since I arrived in the province and I'm, therefore, halfway through my tour. Everything is going well thus far, although we could do with more work. Boredom is one of our most despised enemies. The tedium is broken somewhat when we're called out to deal with a suspect device in Woolworths. It turns out to be a hoax.

Later on, I'm called to deal with a stolen car, which has been dumped along a forestry track. It's been abandoned on the side of a steep hill and, for good measure, it's exposed to half of South Armagh. Since the reason why a car would be abandoned up here isn't clear, the risks are potentially many and the terrorist options varied.

Cars are used extensively by terrorists and clearing them is always problematic since there are many places in which explosives can be concealed. Each incident is unique and has its own idiosyncrasies. On the basis that any damage will write off the car, there's not much point going easy on them – that is, unless

Left: Clearing a crappy old car. Why do we do it? Because we're asked to.

Right: Having attached the rope to the car we're now going to pull the vehicle into cover with our stripped down Land Rover.

there is a good reason to do so, like retaining forensic evidence.

In this event, I decide not to deal with the car out in the open. Instead, I attach a tow rope to it and, with our heli-portable Land Rover, we drag it into tree cover. This is no mean feat, as it doesn't entirely want to come in our direction and there is a danger of it plunging down the hill. In the event, nothing untoward is discovered so the enigma of why it was abandoned miles from anywhere remains. Afterwards, I wonder why I lay my life on the line to clear some crappy old car miles from anywhere, which has already been written off by the insurance company. The answer is: because I was asked to.

28TH FEBRUARY 1981

RPG-7 Rocket Attack, Dundalk Road, Crossmaglen

The austere, bland village of Crossmaglen is situated about 2 km from the border. It is staunchly Republican. At Partition, the populace couldn't believe it when they found that the border would pass to the south of the village and they would remain under British rule. PIRA hasn't let anyone forget this disappointment. It represents the great fault line to both sides. In military

RPG — 7

The rocket propelled grenade RPG 7 is used extensively in the Middle East and is now exported to trouble spots all over the world. No self-respecting group of radicals would be seen without it. This free-flight rocket is highly inaccurate but utilising as it does the explosive 'shaped charge' effect, it has a very effective penetrative capability should it strike a hard target. It will self destruct at about 1000 metres.

circles, Crossmaglen has earned a bloody reputation all of its own.

The police station is now a military fortress. We have abbreviated its name to XMG. This is now an isolated post surrounded by hostile territory. It might not be politically correct to say that, but that's how it is. Everything is helicoptered in and out: policemen, cooks, contractors – even the rubbish. The station has been attacked on multiple occasions with just about everything PIRA could throw at it. There is a good deal in common with what service must have been like on the north-west frontier of India at the turn of the nineteenth century. The facilities are rudimentary to say the least. Some soldiers even live in freight containers. Others live in cramped, smelly squalor, crammed together in submarine bunks, i.e. three bunks high. Even so, morale is a lot higher than you might otherwise imagine. The lads don't do it for the money do they?

Soldiers patrol the streets and border area in multiples of twelve, since smaller numbers are too easily overwhelmed. Armoured vehicles are used to provide support to them but there are no green vehicle movements outside of the immediate village.

I've heard a lot about Crossmaglen and I'm thinking of its grim reputation as my helicopter drops out of the sky like a brick into the police station yard below. The speedy rate of descent makes the machine a harder target for any aspiring sniper. At least that's what I hope.

Today I've been tasked to an RPG rocket and shooting attack on an army patrol. During the attack, the section commander was shot in the chest with a high velocity round. Fortunately, he was wearing a new type of flack jacket and this has saved his life. I don't take too much notice of this as I'm more concerned with getting out on the ground and investigating the explosive aspects of the incident.

I'm told that the rocket was fired at a Saracen armoured vehicle, which had been supporting the foot patrol. It missed, passing overhead, and exploded some way beyond them. It might even have self destructed.

About to leave the police station, I stand behind a 10-ton Saracen armoured car looking at the large wriggly tin gates in front of me. My heart thumps as the gates are pulled back wide. The Saracen kicks into life and the soldiers who will accompany us fan out to the nearest cover quickly, making hard targets of themselves. With their monocular sights, they then scan the streets, roof tops and windows and, in this way, they provide cover for the rest of us.

No one underestimates the dangers of walking out in this place, least of all yours truly!

The Saracen, with its distinct whining engine noise, lurches forward in a burst of blue exhaust fumes and I follow, leaving the relative safety of the fortress behind me. I walk alongside the vehicle as its .30 Browning machine gun swings from side to side and front to back, as if daring anyone to get up to mischief. I look around me at windows and sky lights half-open and my heart is somewhat in my mouth. This isn't something I would want to do too often. The vehicle protects me on one side but not the other. I could sit inside the vehicle but what would that look like! I grit my teeth and plod on. We don't meet many people. Those we do ignore us and they don't hang around, probably not wanting to get caught up in any potential crossfire.

As we progress, I think about one operator, a friend of mine, who had been awarded a medal for gallantry; when called out to support another team in Belfast, he shuddered, took one look at the half-open skylights and got straight back into the vehicle and waited there until he was required. When I saw his fear, I realised that he was probably one of the bravest operators I knew – or perhaps he was just sensible.

British soldiers walk these streets and lanes each and every day and every so often another dies. In one way it's Great Britain, but in another it isn't anything like it.

We move along making good time; soldiers either side of the street move from doorways to gateways, from gateways to garden walls, keeping pace with the Saracen. It's serious stuff – scary. If a car had backfired, I swear I would've had a heart attack! If we're ambushed I have to wonder what contribution I could make, armed, as I am, with only a 9 mm pistol. The only advice I've been given on this so far is, 'Save the last one for yourself, mate!'

We eventually arrive at the outskirts of the village and carry out a search of the area in the vicinity of the telephone exchange. A nose and a tail section of a rocket are found in the vicinity of where it must have exploded. There's no evidence of any damage. Tracing back the likely flight path, we try to find the launch point. This is usually easy to spot due to cardboard debris that's created on firing, but nothing is found. I make a sketch of the area and we then return to the police station the same way we came. I have to say it's a great relief when the gates close behind us.

I leave XMG for Bessbrook by the same Scout helicopter in which I arrived. This chopper provides a taxi service between the two HQs. Because it's pretty much full, I elect to sit on the platform edge with my legs outside the helicopter, feet on the skids. The helicopter stokes up the revs and then lifts off like a rocket, gaining height as fast as possible for all the same reasons as when it arrived. In a couple of seconds, we are at least a hundred or so feet above XMG.

Being perched on the platform, half-in and half-out of the chopper, was a good idea while the helicopter was on the ground, but as it lifts off I realise too late my mistake. The skids move out as the weight is taken off them and my backside leaves the platform. There's a loose webbing strap around me, but it's only the pressure of my boot heels on the pole-shaped skid that is preventing me from dropping out of the helicopter. Panic wells up inside me as I try to get a hold onto the helicopter framework. I shout to the guy next to me to take hold of my jacket, but I'm drowned out by the deafening noise of the engine. The helicopter then banks to the right and I'm overbalancing. Death is imminent. As the devil stares me in the face, someone at last grabs my belt and pulls me back onto the platform. It's not the best, but it'll do!

As I intimated earlier, I don't have a head for heights at the best of times, so the journey back to Bessbrook is still a bloody nightmare. Nonetheless, I arrive there at the same time as the helicopter. If people ever ask me how close I came to being killed in South Armagh, well this incident is right up there.

Under-Car Booby Trap, Millvale Park, Bessbrook

Later that same day, following my traumatic journey from XMG, I'm tasked to a small housing estate just a few hundred yards from Bessbrook Mill. I arrive at 9.40 p.m. and it's dark. In the dimly lit street, I can see a row of white houses about 50 metres away. In front of one house is a Talbot Solara saloon car, which has the driver's door half-open.

The story is that the owner of the Solara is a reserve constable who is based at Bessbrook Police Station and the car is parked outside his house. About to get into his car earlier, he glanced down and spotted a black box underneath the car. The way this is explained, or how I receive it at least, is that the box is on the ground below the driver's seat. This interpretation has unfortunate consequences for our RSP. In the dark, and with high hedges opposite, I'm unable to get into a better position to confirm the exact location of the box and, therefore, I take it as read that it's on the ground.

Everyone has been evacuated from the adjacent houses, so I decide to get on with the job. The Wheelbarrow is tooled up and whirrs off into the darkness towards the car. We peer into the mono TV monitor as it approaches the car. The half-open door of the vehicle comes into view first. Despite some manoeuvring, the door impedes our CCTV view of the car underside. I ask the No. 2 to push the door to, using the Wheelbarrow horizontal boom. He backs up the Wheelbarrow and then moves forward slowly. The boom is raised to the middle of the door and the Wheelbarrow inches slowly forward. Suddenly, 'Bang!' There's a violent explosion, followed almost immediately by the sound of breaking glass and bits of metal clattering to the ground. Everyone leaps against the side of the Transit to shield themselves from the falling debris. Then silence.

What happened? Only now I discover that the box had, in fact, been attached to the car and wasn't on the ground at all. Bugger it! Had I realised this, I would have had us tackle it in a completely different way. The type of device is now blindingly obvious; it's similar to that used to kill the politician Airey Neave in the Houses of Parliament car park.

Hard for me to understand how I didn't ascertain that the device was attached to the car.

The box is clamped on to the car by powerful magnets. With a mercury tilt switch incorporated, it is designed to function as the car moves off. It contains about 3lb of Semtex or a similar type of explosive. Moving the door had unfortunately rocked the car and this was sufficient to trip the tilt switch.

I apologise to the owner for our less than optimum performance. However, he's much more concerned at the closeness of his escape and that of his family. It has also come as a great shock that he's been targeted by PIRA. The family will be relocated immediately. In due course, they'll be compensated for the loss of their car.

Police officers are especially vulnerable to this type of attack. They, and in fact everyone standing up for law and order, are barraged with personal security information to get them to check under their cars when they're left unattended. Too often people think it won't happen to them. He was lucky, but not everyone is.

At this exact moment, we're all pissed off that it got away from us. And I'm particularly galled that I didn't ascertain from my questioning exactly where the thing was located. The explosion has also damaged the Wheelbarrow. This is a shame, because we recently refurbished it with camouflage paint and christened it 'Armageddon' – aptly it now seems. We don't christen any more Wheelbarrows after this. Superstitious? Not a bit of it. I get word that an operator in Belfast, another warrant officer, has been chastised by the SATO for adapting his Wheelbarrow. We're all surprised by this because it has been this type of experiment and innovative thinking that has driven the improvements and modifications to our equipment. It's what got us through the multitude of different situations and scenarios – not any more by the look of it.

The next day, we take a run out to the 3 Brigade Headquarters at Portadown to replace the Wheelbarrow and replenish our explosives and ammunition. At lunch in the Sergeants' Mess, I see a staff sergeant that I think I know from a previous life. This previous life was the apprenticeship I attended at the Army Apprentice College at Chepstow. I remember him as an apprentice corporal in a group a year senior to me. As I have said, there was a pretty strict hierarchy at the college; the more senior groups ruled the more junior groups; there was a lot of 'fagging' and often bullying. I remember him, however, as one of the nicer guys who didn't abuse the power he had. I approach him.

'Excuse me – weren't you at the Apprentice College at Chepstow around 1966? You were an electrician in B Company, Group 66C, I was Group 67B.'

It is Mick Burbridge and we exchange pleasantries about old times and how our military career paths have brought us to this point. He tells me he transferred to the Royal Signals and he's based in Derry and travels around the province in a civilianised vehicle servicing telecommunications equipment. We shake hands and wish each other well. I never expect to meet or hear of him again.

8TH MARCH 1981

Regiments Turnover, Ladies Now Present

The Queen's Lancashire Regiment leave after handing over to the Royal Green Jackets. I'm introduced to the new people we'll be working with. From our perspective, nothing much changes except in one key respect: the RGJ bring with them a troop of female soldiers from the Royal Signals who will 'man' the Telecommunications Centre. The girls are led by a lieutenant of a similar gender.

Females have an impact on the workings of the HQ in a number of ways. Firstly, it is a civilising influence (i.e. there are fewer naked men wandering about the place and the Anglo-Saxon gets toned down a bit). Secondly, the girls become the talk of the town for the chattering classes. Thirdly, the tedious task of washing and drying clothes is now nightmarish; everyone uses the same washing and drying machines. The protocol is that when a machine ends its cycle, the next person empties the contents onto the top of the machine so they can use it. The first time I come across a pile of ladies lingerie I find myself reacting like the stuff is red hot and I hastily beat a retreat. Am I, I wonder, the only one to struggle with this phenomenon? Obviously not, because within a week or so I hear that all the women's underwear has been stolen and it's not hard to imagine by whom. The situation is an emergency – for the girls anyway, who have to send out to Belfast for more. I hope they get compensated. After this, I think they are given their own machines and the guys learn to get their kicks in other ways.

Whether anyone will admit to it or not, tension of a sexual nature now exists in the Mill. Caption competitions are common. These now take on a somewhat lurid note. The lady officer becomes the focus for all the alleged witticisms and – via the Notice Board – receives a barrage of very inappropriate comments, propositions and less-than-covert suggestions. To her credit she seems to take it all in her stride and treats all the unwarranted attention as a joke. Things begin to settle down as everyone gets more used to the new culture, but the underlying pressure remains. Then one day it leaps into focus when I least expect it.

I occasionally drop into the ops room to see if there is any business brewing. Today all is quiet, which I can tell from the minimal radio traffic. Only the ops sergeant appears present and he's manning the radios. From his faraway look and flushed demeanour, however, I can see that something is bothering him; he appears distracted. As I get into the room fully I can see why. In fact, I doubt that he would have heard the mortar alarm had it gone off. I can't fault him, frankly, because I become quickly distracted myself. It's the good lady lieutenant sitting opposite him, passing the time of day and swinging her legs about. Having just played a game of squash by the look of it, she is very fetching in her white kit. This may seem fairly innocuous to people back in Blighty where normality is normal, but not to red-blooded soldiers who are a long way from that place and have been for some time – if you catch my drift. A sentence immediately leaps into my mind that incorporates words like 'very', 'eyes', 'sore' and 'sight'.

Mixing men and women in operational circumstances isn't particularly common in 1981, but it's getting more so. How they'll all cope with the 'it' factor in future is beyond me! I think that preventative action needs to be taken; long bare legs and a short white kit are all very well, but not now; not when we must remain focused on outwitting the enemy and responding quickly to mortar alarms. Someone has to do this and it doesn't look as if the sergeant is making any moves in that direction anytime soon. With a deep breath, I ask her if she's got a minute and take her to one side. In a wholly patronising, but quiet and kindly manner, I whisper that she might want to tone it down a bit. I'll leave it to a psychologist to explain what the 'it' is. A little embarrassed and I expect more knowledgeable as to the complexities and weaknesses of men, she departs the room; sadly, only ever to be seen again in much more sensible clothing. Well, in the ops room at least.

At a later date, during a social call at my office, she gets one over me by drawing attention in a serious manner to the poster on the cabinet that has something to say about fighting for peace and virginity. Amusing as it is, I'm quite embarrassed that she, a female of the lady type, should be exposed to such a profanity.

'I'm sorry, ma'am,' I mumble, somewhat colouring up. My No. 2 abandons me, raising his eyebrows as he goes. There's nowhere to go with this but, seeing my discomfort, she can't keep a straight face and bursts out laughing, as does everyone else. The poster is safe. On operations it isn't just bombs, bullets and dead bodies. Sometimes it can even be a bit of a laugh.

18TH MARCH 1981

Explosion, Louis Boyds Outfitters, Newry

I'm two-thirds through my tour, so it's into the last straight. Over the previous fortnight I've been called to clear a tractor that a farmer was suspicious of and, on another occasion, to destroy an IRA home-made mortar bomb, which had been discovered in a field. Otherwise, business has been slow.

My Royal Sigs ECM expert leaves us at the end of his tour of duty and we welcome his replacement, Kevin Meadows, onto the team.

At 9.00 p.m. on 18th March, two men are seen to hang a blast incendiary device onto the security grill of a men's outfitters in O'Hagen Street. Some fifteen minutes later a warning is telephoned to the police station at Forkhill that a bomb has been left in Newry. The device explodes only five minutes after the warning is given. Fortunately, SF reacted immediately after the men were spotted planting it and the area had been cleared. Otherwise, there could easily have been serious casualties.

'Blue lighting' it to the incident and travelling at speed, we're ambushed by a group of youths gathered at a street corner. They hurl bricks at us as we pass them by. Before the protective metal grill can be pulled up, my Transit windscreen is smashed. Fortunately, the brick doesn't break through the windscreen.

We don't stop. By the time we arrive at the outfitters the fire has been extinguished and the fire brigade are all over the scene. The ground floor of the shop is gutted. There's nothing for me to do except pick up the fragments of device and write my report.

The next day I'm called to clear the car that was used in the attack and, in a separate incident, I'm flown to Forkhill after sparks are reported in a dry stone wall as a soldier climbed over it. Nothing untoward is found at either incident.

24TH MARCH 1981

Scania Truck Clearance, Forkhill

At 10 a.m. I get a call from the ops room. I'm told they're tracking an incident and I may be needed. I place the team on standby. A large Scania truck carrying at least 20 tons of grain had been hijacked the night before. In the events that followed the hijacking, a mechanic from Forkhill was shot in the neck and subsequently died of his wounds in a hospital in Dundalk. Should the truck reappear, I will have to clear it.

I speak with the police liaison officers and the following is what is alleged to have happened: the truck was being used to smuggle grain across the border. When it doesn't arrive at its destination by the due time, the truck owner assumes it has broken down. He drives to Forkhill and picks up his mechanic. From there the pair backtrack the pre-arranged route the truck should have taken. They come across the truck in a narrow country lane but, as they approach, a gunman steps out of the shadows and indicates that they are to stop. Instead, the owner puts his foot down and drives at the gunman who leaps out of the way. The car scrapes down the side of the truck and careers off down the lane. At this point,

SMUGGLING

I'm reliably informed that smuggling is prevalent across the international border. It seems to be a way of life here. With the police restricted in what they can control and customs posts regularly targeted by PIRA, the previous decade has been a bonanza for those so inclined. I surmise that this is one of the main motivations for keeping the conflict going longer than is politically necessary.

a gunman opens fire on them. The car gets through but with the driver shot in the hand. The mechanic is hit in the neck. The car doesn't stop but is driven straight to the hospital in Dundalk.

Meanwhile, the original truck driver is being held hostage in an adjacent field. He's now given a car and told to clear off. Unbeknown to PIRA, he's an ex-member of the Ulster Defence Regiment so he's a very lucky man. In the rear view mirror he sees the truck headlights come on as the truck is started up.

The first anyone at Bessbrook learns of the truck's whereabouts is when the incident is reported on the lunchtime television news. A journalist is giving his report and being filmed next to the truck, which is now parked in a lane near Cortreasla Bridge. The truck seems to have incurred a flat tyre.

An operation is mounted to recover the truck.

Clearing a 30-ton truck so that it can be declared safe isn't easy; there's scope to hide all sorts of things. It's critical, therefore, to get a thorough understanding of exactly what transpired on that fateful night, since this will give me a better understanding of the risks I'm faced with.

We piece the incident together and this is how I come to understand it: The grain was being smuggled across the border via an unapproved crossing. Somehow, the local warlord got wind of it and, not having agreed to the consignment passing through his territory, he had it intercepted. It's likely that the gunmen were waiting for the truck owner to turn up. I think that the hijackers were blinded by the car headlights and didn't know who it was in the car that failed to stop; they shot blindly at it in a fit of pique. With the area compromised they moved the truck to its current location and let its tyre down, still expecting the owner to turn up. When he didn't appear by daylight, they melted away.

This scenario has the ring of truth about it. If so, it is unlikely that much time has been spent by the hijackers preparing anything particularly nasty.

We mount the CCTV camera high and I search the truck the best I can

Getting dressed is at least
a two man task.

Below: LCpl Meadows our new `Bleep'
zips me into the suit.

using the Wheelbarrow. Wearing the IEDD suit, I clear the cab and engine compartment. A driver is eventually sent to move the truck and I have to persuade him it is safe to do so. To give him confidence, I take off the suit and get him to start it up with me standing next to him. I walk alongside as he pulls away. He breathes a sigh of relief when nothing happens. Me too!

We would have towed a much smaller vehicle away from the scene, but this is too big. I have to get on with it. Such an RSP, however, might not have got me through the NI pre-ops course; in theory, there is much that could have gone wrong, but if you try and think of every single scenario the terrorist could cook up you would quickly go mad. Certainly, nothing would get done. The alternative is to destroy every vehicle you're tasked to, just to be safe. As I say, it's important to try and ascertain what the other guys are trying to achieve.

1ST APRIL 1981

A Little Local Pressure?

Following an intelligence tip-off that there is a bomb in the area, Royal Engineer Search teams are tasked to clear a lane near Clontigora. They discover det cord and strips of insulating tape in the road alongside a dry stone wall. No device.

The story is that the locals became unhappy with an ambush bomb that had lain in this position for some time and they were concerned that it might have become unstable. PIRA were informed and removed it for them! I wonder? Not an April fool, surely?

The following year on this date two soldiers are shot and killed, ambushed on their way to repair a telecommunications mast in the Derry area. One of them is the guy I met at Portadown from the Apprentice College at Chepstow. Not just a name on the page this time; not just another statistic. This time, I see the face and hear the voice and I feel the wretchedness of his family deep inside me.

2ND APRIL 1981

Under-Car Explosion

The next day at midnight I'm called to the ops room and notified that an explosion involving a car has occurred in a country lane north of Newry. Green vehicle movements are not banned in that direction and so I decide to travel to the incident via our Transit vehicles.

It's cold, dark, damp and foggy when we set out. Visibility is minimal. We make slow progress. Twenty minutes later we're in the country lane and approaching the rendezvous (RV). Then, in the headlights, we see the white tape strung across the road. We drive up to it and I dismount and look around. It's deathly quiet and very eerie. I notify Bessbrook that we're at the scene, but that no one is present to meet us. Bessbrook confirms that the police are on the ground, so I assume the incident commander is at the other end of the lane.

Taking a torch, I step over the white tape and make my way down the road. It's a 'pea souper' and I'm straining to see into the darkness. Walking down the centre of the road looking forward, I suddenly stumble and realise I've put my foot in a shallow hole. Pointing the torch down I see immediately that it is, in fact, a shallow crater: the seat of an explosion. To the left is a brick wall of a garden, which is peppered and chipped from shrapnel strikes. All around me, I can now see small bits of metal and debris. I walk on. Within a few paces I have to step over identifiable male body parts lying in the road. Then I come across the burnt-out, almost unrecognisable rear section of a car.

Seconds later, I hear voices. Streams of torchlight cut through the mist further down the lane and a number of police officers appear out of the gloom. I introduce myself and the senior police officer explains what he knows.

'It's a bad business this,' he says, but I've already deduced that much. At about 11 p.m. a civilian living in the house adjacent to the crater reported an

A policeman's life cut short.
Another family decimated.

explosion in the road outside. When the agencies arrive, they discover that a Ford Fiesta has blown up and caught fire. The driver is still alive and it turns out he is an RUC constable stationed at Bessbrook Police Station (this is a different establishment to Bessbrook Mill). On completing his duty, the constable had collected his car from the nearby housing estate and driven home. He routinely parked in the housing estate because Bessbrook Police Station doesn't have its own car park! This is a shock to me; the risk to police officers working at that establishment is so blindingly obvious.

Because he was conscious when taken away in the ambulance, the senior police officer is optimistic about the policeman's chances. From what I have seen in the road, however, I am fairly certain he isn't going to make it and to reduce his expectations I say so. Sadly, the guy died en route to the hospital.

Piecing this incident together, I conclude that the device was fitted to the car shortly before the constable arrived at it. This type of device has a timer incorporated, which provides the bomber with a delay before it arms. The timer was, therefore, in all likelihood, still running when the constable got into the car. Some ten minutes later, the device armed and the car's movements simultaneously triggered the firing circuit. Travelling at speed, probably before the mist came down, the car broke up and burst into flames.

This device would have been similar to the one we dealt with four weeks previously. Tragically, the constable had not checked under his car and this cost him his life.

15TH APRIL 1981

Blast Incendiary, Norbrook Laboratories

Business is slow. In the previous period I've only had to deal with a couple of incidents that both turned out to be false alarms. They prevented us from getting too bored at least. Then, at midnight on 15th April, an explosion is reported at the Norbrook Pharmaceutical Laboratory in Newry. The explosion has gutted the first floor of the building. A further device is reported by the owner. It's been placed in a sterilisation room and, from its description, it's a blast incendiary.

At the laboratory I find that the Wheelbarrow can't be used, because there are too many doors to negotiate and these would trap the umbilical cord. A manual approach is therefore necessary. I get dressed in the IEDD suit and my No. 2 primes a Disrupter and fits it into its purpose-built stand.

Armed also with a sketch of the room and floor layout, I walk into the building and through the final door. There it is, staring at me. To all intents and purposes, it's exactly the same as the device at the Killeavy truck yard; the dowel pin, however, isn't present this time. The can has all the same possibilities.

I place the Disrupter muzzle within an inch or two of the TPU and leave the room. The Disrupter will pretty much disintegrate the wooden box but, unfortunately, there's nothing in my armoury that is less powerful. If I use some other technique or try to be innovative I'll be right in the shit from you-know-who if it goes wrong. Despite the low probability of anything going wrong, I can't risk it.

Bang! the Disrupter is fired. I give it a few minutes and re-enter the room. The TPU and the can are both smashed and it takes only a second or so to make sure all the bits of device remaining are completely separated out. Satisfied that the device is safe, I go to collect the Disrupter but find that it's missing from the stand – there's no sign of it. I'm puzzled and I look around the floor but, sure enough, it's gone. I take off my helmet and then I see that the electrical firing cable is hanging from the ceiling next to the entrance. The Disrupter has recoiled out of the stand and penetrated right through the ceiling.

I pull on the cable to recover the Disrupter. I should have been wearing the helmet, because half the bloody ceiling plaster comes crashing down onto my head. Brilliant! When I come out of the building I look like Mr Pastry!

18TH APRIL 1981

Kidnapping, Jonesborough

On 18th April we're flown to Jonesborough: a town that straddles the border on the east of our area. A farm labourer is reported to have been kidnapped by armed men, probably PIRA. His car has since been spotted in the town. It's located within a few metres of the border. We need to be clear about where the border is for obvious reasons and I'm amazed to find that it passes through the middle of an adjacent farmyard. There's nothing on the ground to distinguish the border at all. Highly porous is one way of describing it. But, to me, it exists merely to constrain the activities of the security authorities on both sides of the fence. The RUC do liaise with the Garda, fortunately, and the latter are in evidence on their side of the border throughout the operation. Because we aren't allowed over the border, however, the Royal Engineer Searchers have to pass within 25 metres of the car in their search for buried command wires. This is not ideal.

The two police forces seem to be quite relaxed with each other, but it is less than politically correct for the Garda to liaise directly with the British Army.

Using the shotgun fitted to the Wheelbarrow, we open up the car bonnet and then the boot. I half expect to find either a body or a bomb, but there's neither.

I don the IEDD suit and approach the car. Judging by the amount of straw and farmyard debris present, the owner must have kept pigs or cattle in it. A

Half the farm buildings are in the south, half are in the north. The suspect vehicle can be seen on the right.

BORDER - EIRE

jacket lies on the back seat and I check it out. I'm amazed to find that the pockets are stuffed with wads of money – Irish punts. How he came by that amount of money I do not know. Perhaps it's a clue to what's happened to the owner. The money might be the profit from some nefarious activity that has come to the attention of PIRA. In South Armagh, apparently, they see themselves as public protectors when it suits them. Anyway I can only surmise and I pass it all to the RUC for safe keeping.

A couple of days later, I hear that the lad has been set free by his kidnappers having been given, I guess, the fright of his life.

19TH APRIL 1981

Attack on Warrenpoint Police Station

It's the following day and late evening when I'm called to the ops room for a task briefing. I'm told that a van parked opposite the police station at Warrenpoint has roused police suspicions. The RUC are carrying out more checks, but it looks serious. We are to move out at 2 a.m. under additional escort. In the meantime, we should get some rest as it's going to be a long night. I try to get some sleep, but it's impossible.

We move out on time. In order to avoid the possibility of ambush, we take a circuitous route to the town of Warrenpoint. As the convoy rolls in, it's cold and misty and the streets are empty and silent. At the corner of the main street we're met by a police officer who is our contact. Together, we peer around the corner and he points out the police station about 100 metres away. Its frontage is illuminated by a variety of bright security lights. Around the building are the concrete blocks linked by steel poles, which are used everywhere to prevent car bombs from being placed too close to buildings, thereby limiting the structural damage they can cause. The police officer points out the suspicious Ford Escort van, which is easy to see, parked as it is all alone on the opposite side of the wide street.

The police officer brings me up to speed on the story so far. A farmer known to the police always parks his van in that spot on market days – nothing suspicious there. However, when the vehicle was still there at 10 p.m. the police telephoned the owner at his home to ask why he hadn't taken it away. The farmer replied that his van was, in actual fact, parked out the front of his house. A police patrol was quickly diverted to the farm and, sure enough, what the farmer had said was confirmed. The van at the police station was, therefore, bogus. It had been twinned (i.e. re-sprayed and fitted with a number plate the same as the farmer's).

What then follows is either heroic or foolish, others can decide. Before my arrival, the police allow a constable to conduct a rather alarming and risky reconnoitre of the van. Putting on a civilian jacket and waving an empty beer bottle, he staggers and swayed his way up the main street pretending to be a drunk. Arriving at the van, he rolls onto the bonnet and then having peered inside, continues to amble on up the road until he is far enough away to be safe. The constable is now able to inform me that, 'The van's empty except for a narrow roll of old carpet across the back doors'.

If PIRA's intention is to attack the police station then an empty van doesn't stack up. But the police station isn't the only potential target; PIRA has clearly gone to a lot of trouble to arrange this and there are a variety of places where a device can be hidden in a van. An anti-handling switch is an obvious option, but there could still be a timer running down on us. Both are easily feasible. Another likely option is that the device is radio controlled (RC). If so, we can be certain that the terrorist is watching the scene even now from a vantage point somewhere in the vicinity. If it is RC, the bomber might fire the device if he suspects we've sussed his plan. As we're some distance away and around the corner, we might assume he doesn't know we're on to him just yet.

After a quick discussion with my Royal Sigs ECM expert, we conclude that the best way of dealing with this is to drive the ECM Transit vehicle forward with the ECM equipment transmitting white noise. This is called the direct approach; the electronic field we transmit can be expected to confuse a radio control receiver. The hope is that the bomber, seeing us approaching, might initially think we're driving into his killing zone. When we're about 50 or so metres from the suspicious van, we'll swing the vehicle across the road and this will become the IEDD control point. Troops will pan out and secure the area. Even if the bomber realises then that we're on to him and tries to transmit a firing signal, the radio control receiver by then won't be able to pick out the firing signal. Any such device will, therefore, be under our control. That's the plan anyway.

The police and troops are briefed. The ECM equipment is switched on and we take a break as it has to warm up. Suddenly, there's a muffled 'thump': a sound like a low velocity gun shot. Somebody speaks for all of us: 'What the f*ck was that?' For a second, there's confusion and everyone goes to cover.

A policeman appears and tells me he thinks the sound came from the van. I peer around the corner of the building and, using the binoculars, study the van. There's no sign that anything has changed – no smoke, broken glass or anything untoward. I have my suspicions, but not enough to change the plan.

We move off with me walking alongside the front vehicle. We're quite exposed in the middle of the street and there's no additional security at this point, so

It's cold and quiet and the van opposite the police station has been `twinned`. I take aim at the rear windows with the shotgun and I'm probably much too close.

Right: The small explosive charge rang out in the empty street and the photographer clearly jumped out of his skin.

it's a little unnerving to think we're possibly being watched by PIRA from a skylight or window. Approximately 50 metres from the van, I tell the driver to swing the vehicle across the street. At this point, troops from either end of the street appear and seal it off. The suspect van is now well within the range of our ECM equipment, so hopefully we are in control of any RC switch. There are no occupied houses within the immediate vicinity, so no one to evacuate.

With the area now secured by the SF, we can get on with the clearance. I take our Browning shotgun and shoot out the rear windows of the van. Using the RCV Wheelbarrow, we manoeuvre into position a 2 oz explosive charge inside and to the centre of the vehicle. After giving a warning, the charge is fired and the sharp bang echoes up and down the empty streets. The violent over-pressure completely detaches the van roof and throws open the rear doors – perfecto! The explosion wakes up the whole town and also the fire alarm in the fire station at the other end of the street. It's a hell of a din. Retained firemen suddenly appear from a variety of doors pulling jackets over pyjamas and we watch as they rush in to report for duty.

With the smoke cleared, we move in again with the Wheelbarrow CCTV. We pan the camera left and right. In the grainy mono picture we can see a spare tyre and some tools, but there's little else to raise our suspicions. Using the binoculars, I can make out the roll of carpet hanging half-in and half-out of the rear doors, but the situation remains unsettling and is far too ambiguous for my liking. There's nothing for it, however, but to approach the van and eyeball it.

As I get ready to approach the van, the questions in my head are: Where did that earlier explosion arise from? Has a timer expired and fired a detonator or could our ECM equipment have inadvertently initiated something? Has the terrorist tried to initiate it but failed?

With a torch, I walk up to the rear of the van and peer in. I see the back of both driver and passenger seats. There's nothing suspicious in the cargo area. It's empty like the constable said but, pointing the torch down, I see something familiar, which was missed with the CCTV; it's whitish.

'Bloody hell – det cord!'

A length of it runs from between the front seats along the floor of the van towards me. I look down at the roll of carpet next to my leg and then my heart skips a few beats! Yes, there is an old rug, but it's wrapped around a metal gas cylinder which is looking an awful lot bigger than it did when it was purely a rug ten or so minutes ago. It's quite a shock! When my heart starts up again, it's pounding like a good'n.

I gather my thoughts and contemplate whether discretion would indeed pass for the better part of valour. I decide to tough it out. Walking to the front of the vehicle, I shine the torch into the passenger well. I see the electronic switching arrangement contained in an open Tupperware box. I can also see the remains of detonator leads. The detonator has indeed fired, but this hasn't propagated to the 40 lb of high-explosives in the gas cylinder and it isn't hard to see why. The Det Cord is comprised of bits, taped together to make a long length. The end of it is shattered where it has failed to pick up the blast wave when the detonator functioned. All the elaborate planning that PIRA must have put into this attack has been let down by poor quality explosives.

The switch is contained in the box with a large blue battery and is, indeed, radio controlled. I recover the container. Our operating instructions oblige me to notify CATO or SATO of any incident involving radio controlled switches, so I try. Unfortunately, I can't use my PYE radio because we're out

The 'small' gas cylinder lies in the street behind the shattered van after IEDD action.

Left: The proximity of the van to the fortified police station can be seen here.

Below: The van after the clearance.

Below: Wicks and I empty the explosives from the cylinder.

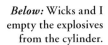

Above Right: The 40lbs of explosives would have made a mess of anyone in the vicinity of the police station.

Right: The Radio Control Switch and battery recovered with the Tupperware container.

of range of HQ Bessbrook, never mind Lisburn. Instead, I ask the incident commander if he would kindly notify ops at Bessbrook with his more powerful radio and relay a message to my bosses for me. I naively think it will get through.

Dawn is breaking as we clear up and bag the forensic evidence. Everyone is weary now and there is nothing to be gained from hanging around Warrenpoint town centre as the town wakes up. I decide to take the team back to Bessbrook. Given the circumstances, I think that everything has gone pretty well, except that I realise now that I'm much too susceptible to autosuggestion. When someone tells me something and there's no reason to believe otherwise, I accept it at face value. This phenomenon also occurred at the under-car booby trap at Millvale Park. It's a weakness in my questioning technique.

You do your best. You think you have a handle on it, but there is this great potential to be caught out. Most survive these aberrations – some die.

At Bessbrook there's no sign of the SATO, so I telephone him. The call wakes him up, which is the first inkling I have that communications haven't gone according to plan.

'Did you get the message I relayed to you, sir?'

He hasn't. He asks what it's all about. I begin to explain the incident but, as soon as he hears the words 'RC device', he becomes enraged. My heart sinks. He yells down the phone, calling me a women's body part. He offers me no further chance to explain and, after some other equally flowery expletives, he slams the phone down. It's a real pity the call wasn't recorded, you know, for training purposes.

I brace myself for the storm to come and he gets to Bessbrook in record time. The wheels must have hardly touched the tarmac. Now, most people might be pleased the job had been completed safely. Not this guy – he has a face like thunder. If it wasn't before, I can see it's definitely personal now. He's affronted, mainly because an RC device should have been his shout – passed to him. He wants to speak with me alone.

Finding an empty office, he begins what quickly becomes an interrogation. He states that I've deliberately disobeyed standing orders by not calling him out earlier. He begins to tear me apart. He doesn't shout, but his words are like vitriol. He's driving in nails. He isn't interested in the complexity or the ambiguous nature of the task. He doesn't like the approach I took, the type of explosive weapon I used, the point that we switched on the electronic counter measures. Nothing I say makes any sense to him. He broadens his attack into my general abilities as a warrant officer, which, if true, should have been raised before now. For forty-five minutes I endure what I believe is mainly petulance. In the army, you can't walk with your feet; you have to bear it, even if you're having trouble with the grin.

Any residual respect I might have had for the guy evaporates that night. With no sleep, I'm exhausted. The adrenalin has long since worn off. I'm struggling to take most of it in. I feel the black dog of depression barking. Finally he's finished, ending with a swan song around, 'I should have you replaced.' Having been forewarned at the beginning of the tour hadn't helped me to prepare for this.

Later, he takes hold of the forensic evidence and begins to pull it apart, as he did at the Chancellors Road incident. From across the room, I watch him remove components to examine them. Also watching this, the RUC Border Superintendent takes me to one side and tells me the SATO has probably ruined the forensic evidence. It's now inadmissible in court. But he's talking to the wrong guy. I tell him I'm not best placed to deal with it. I ask the super to speak to him himself. Whether he does or not, I don't know. To be honest, I'm beyond caring. I feel physically sick.

My difficult relationship with the SATO has finally erupted. At the team room it's hard to hide that I'm gutted. Initially, they're confused, but then begin to ask whether what we are doing is safe. They question me. They begin to doubt. Who can blame them since decisions I make could obviously have consequences for them? They're also concerned as to whether they might be implicated in any fallout. Both times they've seen the SATO he hasn't had a good word to say to them. This matter becomes a complete distraction, which has more in keeping with what you might have expected in the Crimean War than a modern army. But, in reality, all life exists here as it does in any other walk of life.

After a couple of days mulling it over, I can't put the issue out of my head. The matter is eating away at me. I'm depressed – or, in the army vernacular, 'seriously pissed off'. The team remains twitchy and uncertainty reigns supreme. I decide to take the matter to the only other person I can realistically take it to – the CATO.

I telephone HQ 321 at Lisburn. Unfortunately, the CATO isn't in and so I'm put through to – guess who? I'm on the spot now.

He wants to know why I've asked to see the CATO. I tell him that, given everything he's said to me, I feel I'm entitled to speak with the commanding officer. Of course my mistake is like a red rag to a bull and his reaction is pretty predictable. I begin to wonder if he's actually lost the plot. I don't even know if my request to see the CATO is passed through.

Three weeks pass following the Warrenpoint RC task. The team and I soldier on. I'm fed up, bad tempered and touchy, and this has its negative impact on the team. The situation is crap, but then a soldier's life often is.

All goes quiet on the Bessbrook front. PIRA are probably taking stock of their failures and organising the next big thing. The hunger strikes at Long Kesh Prison are drawing to their inevitable conclusion and PIRA won't want to draw attention away from this. Finally, on 5th May, Bobby Sands dies after a hunger strike lasting sixty-six days. There's rioting elsewhere in the province but, despite us anticipating it, his death doesn't bring us any immediate business. It's just a matter of time, however.

8TH MAY 1981

'Contact' on the Border

Over the intervening period, I deal with two minor incidents, which turn out to be false alarms.

On 8th May I'm tasked to attend a follow-up to an incident which has occurred on the border and has involved the COP. The story is that when the incident occurred the platoon was asleep in their daytime hide, having been out on the ground the night previously. Their bored sentry crawled forward to a rise and, to his amazement, came across four armed and masked men moving away from him in file along the border. The distance was less than 50 metres. Scurrying back and waking the rest of the group, he returned in time to open up on them as they disappeared into 'dead' ground. The fire fight which resulted went on for some considerable time and much ammunition was expended. Eventually, one terrorist, trying to make his escape, found himself trapped in the corner of a dry stone wall on the other side of the border. The COP machine gunner tried his best to demolish the wall, but no luck, and the guy was fortunate enough to be arrested by the Garda before the wall completely collapsed. Another guy was discovered cowering in a ditch on our side of the border and was taken into custody. Found to be lying on a very nice Heckler Koch automatic rifle, he's lucky he wasn't shot. So, if there is a shoot to kill policy in force in the province – you know, like PIRA's – well, someone should have told our boys. Two baddies managed to escape.

The Border area where a PIRA unit was intercepted by the Close Observation Platoon. The ensuing fire fight went on across the border for quite some time before two of them were finally arrested and taken into custody.

I make safe the abandoned weapons and bomb components they'd been carrying. Whatever it was they had planned to carry out, it had been well thwarted. Incidents like this are good for the troops' morale.

Later that day, I'm called to clear a car that the Garda believe was driven by the PIRA unit involved in the contact. They think it might be booby trapped. It isn't.

Mortar Attack, Newtownhamilton

The 8th May has already been a busy day when, at 8.30 p.m. an infantry officer bursts through the office door and exclaims, 'Felix, can you come to the ops room now? NTH is under attack.' He's excited and this is always contagious.

'NTH' is the abbreviation for the military barracks and combined police station at Newtownhamilton. An infantry platoon is located there and covers the far west of our tactical area.

As we approach the ops room I ask the officer when the attack happened.

'It's still happening,' he says.

'Bloody hell!' I reply.

The burst of adrenalin can almost make you dizzy!

When we enter the ops room, the RGJ commanding officer is present and the radio traffic is hot. He says, 'Newtownhamilton has been mortared, Felix. There are casualties. I'm going up there now. Hopefully, the area will have been secured by the time we get there. Do you want a lift?'

I reply that I would.

He adds, 'Are you ready? We're leaving now.'

I race back to my office to collect my pistol and flack jacket with just enough time to brief the team. I finish with, 'Follow me up in the vehicles. I'll meet you there.' Then I'm off.

Sometimes you don't have much time to think, so planning is rudimentary. Your responses or choices, however, are limited despite what may be suggested on the NI pre-ops IEDD course. In the real world, you make decisions as the incident unfolds around you. Rules can only be a guide; tolerance is needed. Paramount is providing everyone with confidence that you are the person to deal with it and that you are not hindered by a bureaucracy they don't understand.

As we approach NTH, the Gazelle helicopter drops down through the clouds. There's no sign of a fire, no smoke. The helicopter bumps down into the playing fields across the road from the base and we pile out. It immediately lifts off – too much of a target to hang around.

Two soldiers appear from the side of a building; one of them is an officer, the other (with a rifle) is his escort. The officer greets the CO and we're told

PIRA HOME-MADE MORTAR BOMBS

The mortar bombs currently in use by PIRA are large steel cylinders with fins, each of which contains up to 40lbs of HME. The bomb has a range of a couple of hundred yards. PIRA use this weapon because it isn't constrained by standard fortifications. It provides them with a means of lobbing explosives over the highest walls.

to move quickly – the area isn't yet secure. I follow them and we scurry across the main road into the relative safety of the barracks. Once behind the blasted wriggly tin walls, I can see that an accommodation block is very badly damaged. The air is still thick, almost toxic, with dust and the telltale smell of blasted HME. A soldier passes us piggy backing another who has a bandage around his head and looks semiconscious. Another holding a rifle is wearing carpet slippers, no flack jacket. Clearly, he's had to get out in a hurry.

We press on to the ops room where the staff explain what has occurred so far. A Tipper lorry was being watched via the CCTV as it approached along the main road that passes by the base. Nothing odd with that, but then it stopped 100 metres away. At this point, the driver was seen to dismount and disappear across the street. Almost immediately, a small explosion was heard and the first mortar bomb was projected into the sky. This took with it the black polythene tarpaulin that had disguised the lorry contents from the air. Accordingly, the bomb fell short and exploded in the street. Then, salvos of mortar bombs were seen on the CCTV erupting from the vehicle and hurtling towards them, smoke streaming from their tails. Most landed within the barracks but one overshot and hit a house.

Soldiers, who were quickly deployed to secure the helicopter landing area, were then fired on from the far side of the playing fields. One of the soldiers had a close escape. He shows me a bullet lodged in the heel of his boot.

The SF accommodation block destroyed by PIRA mortar bombs.

Most of the bombs have hit and demolished the soldiers' accommodation block, which, by an act of God, was mainly empty at the time. The accuracy of the attack has been uncanny. Amazingly, the Security Forces haven't suffered any fatalities, but casualties are still being tended to. One shocked soldier, still hyper, recounts to me how he dived to the floor of his room when he heard the first explosion, at which point a mortar bomb crashed through the roof and embedded itself in the floor in front of him. He describes the tail fins to me. With just enough time to lift himself up and throw himself out of the room, the bomb exploded. He found himself on the ground floor, dazed but unhurt. Fortunately for him, this type of mortar bomb has a timer rather than an impact fuze.

Twenty minutes after the first mortar left the truck a separate explosion occurred in the truck cab and demolished it.

I look into the grainy mono screen of the ops room CCTV monitor; the truck is clearly visible. When I messed up the mortar job at the NI pre-ops course, I had it drilled into me that I must quickly ascertain the status of the firing platform. The big question is, have all the mortars fired? People are out in the open and a further salvo of mortars could have catastrophic consequences. I need to check this out, and quick, so I need to see into the truck.

Because the area is still not fully secure, I'm provided with an armed escort. The two of us make our way to the main road. I have no equipment with me. I climb onto a garage roof nearby, but I still can't see into the high-sided truck. There's nothing else for it but to get onto the truck itself. Now this puts me in a dilemma. Operating procedures state that a set time should elapse before a manual approach is attempted in case of secondary devices. That duration has not yet passed. The alternative is to escalate the matter to SATO/CATO for permission to approach the target within the time period. Well, at the moment I'm standing on a garage roof without any communications. There's no time to make the call. No time to wait. I haven't time to explain the ins and outs to SATO. But I hesitate because this could be the man's chance to get shot of me. Should I cover myself? Should I return to the ops room and

The truck abandoned in the main street.

refer the matter up? What if I appear in a newspaper photograph? For the first time in the tour, I'm indecisive, I'm struggling. I'm thinking about personal consequences, not getting on with the job! Then I say out loud. 'F*ck it!' I decide to go for it regardless. It frees me from the indecision. Any arguments can be had afterwards.

I get hold of a ladder and make my way to the truck. Placing the ladder against the side, I shimmy to the top and look down into it. Bolted to the base is the heavy metal framework that supports the large metal firing tubes. I scan each tube. They all seem empty but then – 'Shit!' – one tube muzzle is capped. This is not what I had expected to see. Either they would all be empty or, if not, the forward part of a bomb would be protruding from the tube. This one is different. Questions fill my mind. Could it be a different type of mortar bomb? Should I get down there and remove the cap? Is there some way I can prevent it from firing? I can't see a firing cable or a switch. Is it about to fire or

The cab has been destroyed by a blast incendiary device. The ladder remains by which I and the CATO scaled the sides.

is it a device that might explode? Too many questions for which there are no answers. I'm already out on a limb. Indecision returns. I withdraw.

Back at the ops room now, everyone is notified of the potential situation. Extra care is to be taken. People are to remain under hard cover unless absolutely necessary. I await the arrival of my team. As time progresses, the likelihood of it being a live mortar bomb diminishes.

Then the CATO arrives on the scene. I brief him on the position as it stands. He decides to approach the truck. Climbing down into the truck, he pulls off the cap. It's comprised of melted residue from the polythene tarpaulin. The tube's empty. He declares the truck clear. It's safe.

I go on to inspect the remainder of the truck. The damage to the cab has all the hallmarks of a blast incendiary device. If their intention had been to destroy the mortar firing switches, they failed because the crate containing all the switches has been thrown out into the road. I recover all the components intact. I'm amazed at how 'Heath Robinson' the switching arrangements are. It's been assembled in a great hurry, that's obvious. The electric cables are like

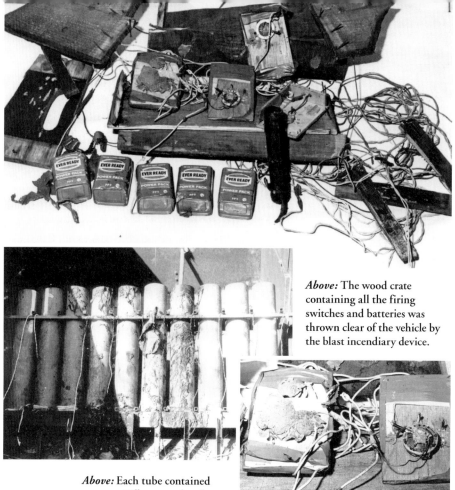

Above: The wood crate containing all the firing switches and batteries was thrown clear of the vehicle by the blast incendiary device.

Above: Each tube contained an 80lb mortar bomb.

Above: Having been assembled in a real hurry, the switches are pretty rough and ready. If wire cutting is your preferred modus operandi, well there's plenty to choose from here.

spaghetti and the car body filler that glues it all together looks as if it's been splashed into place with a paddle. Nonetheless, I can't fault them on the fact that the switches did the job they were meant to and all the mortars fired.

The postscript to this incident is that the Royal Engineers work hard throughout the night and repair the outer fencing. The next day there's no sign of the extensive damage to the barracks. The attack doesn't even get a mention in the TV News, thus denying PIRA any kudos from all the planning and effort that must have gone into mounting it. I think we score this one as even.

I take the opportunity to speak privately with the CATO with reference to my deteriorating relationship with the SATO. At this point, I'm not even sure if the CATO's aware of it. I'm hyped up after weeks of sitting on it and also seriously pissed off that I had to make decisions today based not on what I thought was right, but on what the SATO's reaction might have been. The

CATO knows something is going on and I suspect there are problems elsewhere in the unit. He isn't prepared to discuss the SATO, however, as that would be bad form. Nonetheless, he goes as far as he can. He's personally very happy with the way things are at the section and he's had good reports from the people I work with. He wants things to continue as they are. Well, that's good enough for me. It's the endorsement I need to get mentally back on the case. It may be a cliché, but the great weight that lifted off my shoulders at that moment was almost discernible.

Later, I get the team together and I pass on the CATO's words. I reassure them we aren't doing anything we shouldn't. I tell them it's a matter between the SATO and I. It's not perfect by any means. It never could be and I still have a bad taste in my mouth, but it'll do. Things calm down.

The day after the mortar attack, I am asked to clear a military Storno radio that has been found by a civilian at Newtownhamilton and handed in. The radio is a solid state type of technology. I check it out and it's clear. I then have an argument with the 321 Senior Ammunition Technician from Lisburn as to whether I dealt with it appropriately. I know from rumours that he's under pressure to be more exacting and challenging with operators in respect of their Render Safe Procedures. I have to justify to him every action I took. We get into a silly discussion, which is unprofessional in my opinion. 321 isn't a particularly happy ship at this time.

The New Flack Jacket

Later in the day, the team is issued with the new flack jackets. These have, what I consider, relatively small titanium plates fitted front and back. This jacket is designed to stop high-velocity bullets and not just fragmentation, like its predecessor. Unlike its predecessor, this jacket is worn underneath the combat jacket. As with anything new, there are the critics and it's hard to get

The high-velocity strike mark can be seen on the plate

ecstatic about anything that's bulky, heavier than its predecessor and limits your movements somewhat. It doesn't look cool either, as it gives you a distinct Quasimodo appearance.

In Crossmaglen, however, when a foot patrol of the RGJ is fired upon from a school about a hundred yards away, both lead soldiers are hit dead centre with high-velocity rounds. As one falls he's skimmed by another potentially fatal shot. The titanium plates in both jackets absorb the impact of the rounds and both soldiers suffer only minor injuries. A miracle?

I now recollect the RPG rocket attack back in February, where the section commander's life was also saved by this model of jacket. From here on in, the new flack jackets have very few detractors – especially me.

A 'Force' to be Reckoned with

I've struck up a friendship with the RGJ Regimental Sergeant Major, RSM Goddard. He's a nice bloke; I enjoy his company and the team like him too. He accompanies us on jobs, thus providing us with additional protection. People often like to accompany us as they're pretty much guaranteed a bit of excitement! However, a different type of excitement arrives at Bessbrook Mill in the shape of an MoD-sponsored Combined Services Entertainment (CSE) show. One act among many is a trio of pretty female dancers who call themselves 'Dee Force'. Eagerly awaited by the troops, they do their sexy thing to very loud music and roars of appreciation. Watching them wearing not too much diminishes all thoughts of terrorist bombs and frankly everything else that isn't directly in the line of sight. Their gyrations begin to imbue in me all-too-familiar physiological feelings. Yes, that's right; there are clear and recognisable similarities to how

I feel when approaching a device! My pulse rate has increased, adrenalin is flowing, body temperature is rising and my palms sweat. But this time it's actually uncomfortable, even stressful. IEDs are hazardous, but beware a trio of bikini-bottomed bombshells in black satin basques!

After the show, the

Warrant Officers' and Sergeants' Mess hosts a dinner to which all the entertainers are invited. The RSM sees to it that I have pride of place seated alongside our very attractive lady guests. They're good fun, chatty and a very welcome relief from the green routine. Later at the bar, the girls show us they're still wearing stockings. Excellent! Some distractions up with, they just have to be put!

Towards the end of the dinner, the decanter of port is circulated and all glasses charged for the loyal toast. This is a toast to Her Majesty the Queen and a tradition in every regiment. I'm somewhat amazed when the loyal toast is given that all the soldiers remain seated. I turn to a warrant officer nearby and query this. 'Isn't that disrespectful to the Queen?' He replies, as he probably has had to do on many occasions, 'Our loyalty was never in doubt.' The idiosyncrasies and traditions of the British Army regimental system – wonderful!

19TH MAY 1981

Group Photograph – Fatal Timing

Rear - Moggy Wolstenholme, Cyril Simpson, Steve Turner.
Front - Davy Marshall, Paul Wharton, Superintendent Caldwell

I deal with two more minor incidents in the interim – a hoax and a false alarm. These keep us on our toes but my mind is beginning to think of other things –

handover and home. I arrange for a photograph to be taken of the people I've worked with so closely: the RUC Border Superintendent, the two RUC Liaison Officers, the Royal Engineer Search Adviser and my No. 2 (whose tour is also complete, hence the civvies). The camera clicks; we stand and begin to put the chairs away. Then, suddenly, 'Baboom!' The unmistakeable thump of a very large explosion shakes the ground. It reverberates and echoes all around the hills...

Explosion, Culvert, Chancellors Road, Bessbrook

I make my way quickly to the ops room. Already, the radio traffic is hot. The ops officer tells me what he knows. Two Saracen armoured vehicles of support company making their way down the Chancellors Road to the Dundalk Road have been attacked. The second vehicle has been hit. It is carrying five soldiers.

I suggest to him that the armoured nature of the vehicle may have protected the soldiers but, from the reports he's receiving, the officer is dubious.

The army doctor is quickly on the ground and, without any regard to his own safety, is reported as running to and fro like a mad man, up and down the area, left and right to try and locate the soldiers in case any are in need of help. This (and what he eventually confirms) is grim.

I call HQ Lisburn and inform the CATO of what I know. I tell him I need to get to the incident immediately. He says he'll meet me there.

Within fifteen minutes, I'm in a helicopter over the scene. A massive scar across the whole of the road is unmistakable. The crater must be 50ft across and at least 15ft deep. I thought I would see an armoured vehicle in the vicinity of the crater, but of this there is no sign. I need to get on the ground quickly, as the incident is already gaining momentum and there are potential dangers from secondary devices.

ON WHOM THE DUST HAS SETTLED

The pitch and yaw of spinning blades
skim us fevered o'er the rolling mounds.
As sunshine bakes the greeny glades
we find the blasted ground.
A leafy lane that's ended,
its tarmac shredded and torn.
The fractured earth and shattered steel heap
shame on an Irish dawn.

Hovering over the morbid scene
look, listen, no one need speak.
For no one heard a final scream
for when death came, it came too quick

Mourn then our five young warriors
now bathed in dappled shades.
On whom the dust has settled
amid Armagh's greeny glades

We approach the RV by vehicle from the south after all the culverts have been searched. The press and TV teams are beginning to arrive. An apparent lack of compassion for what we are dealing with here is hard for me to stomach and I insist to the police that they move them way back, well away from the scene. None of us want morbid pictures appearing in the newspapers. We wait by our Transit vehicles as the Royal Engineer Search Teams carry out a 360-degree sweep of the area. Very soon a command wire is detected running up the side of the hill towards a housing estate. As I await the go-ahead to enter the scene and clear the crater of any residual explosives, a light aeroplane circles above us. The next day, I know why when photographs of the scene appear on the front page of all the leading newspapers.

Right: The beginning of the rubble can just be seen at the bend in the lane.

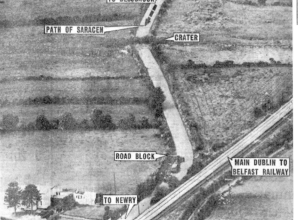

Left: The *Daily Mail* aerial photograph of the scene.

It isn't long before the CATO arrives on the scene and I receive a message to say that he's gone straight to the terrorist firing point, which has been located by the Royal Engineers. He asks for some of our equipment to deal with a battery pack that has been found there. I'm about to approach the seat of the explosion, so I'm not overly happy about this and I also happen to think he's acting somewhat impatiently considering that the last culvert device I dealt with also had a booby trapped battery pack. However, I'm not going to argue. I have some equipment sent to him and he recovers the battery pack and its integral bell push switch, fortunately, without any further drama. We recover the terrorist command wire, which is approximately 500 metres long and buried along its whole length to a depth of about 6 inches. Most of the wire had been in place for at least six months. When I eventually get to the terrorist firing point, it is plain to see that the bomber had been sitting in front of a hedge watching the road for quite some time, judging by the number of cigarette butts lying around. He let the first vehicle through before pressing the bell push switch. The immediate event would have been the sight of tons of earth and the disintegrating vehicle lifting skywards. This followed within a second by the 'Kaboom!' of the pressure wave travelling at probably 3,000 metres a second, echoing around the hills. Then everything would have gone into slow motion as the debris reached its zenith and began to fall back to earth. He may have heard the thud as the few remaining vehicle parts of any size struck the ground. As the dust cloud reached 100 feet, he would already have turned his back on the scene and started making his way quickly to his getaway car. It was all over in seconds – no fire, no flame, only a massive scar across the landscape pinpointing the tragedy that had just been played out. How many people in the housing estate saw him? I wonder – the only person moving in the opposite direction.

Two years earlier, one of our teams was attacked in this way whilst on their way to an incident. Similarly, the second vehicle was taken out and the Royal Signals ECM specialist and his escort were both killed.

The Royal Engineers sweep around the area. But, before the dead can be removed, we need to be safe and I ensure that the immediate area of the crater is free from explosives.

The explosion has been massive. The device contained a similar amount of explosives to that used in the Chancellors Road culvert device we dealt with last February. This size is pretty much confirmed when another bomb disposal team, based at Aughnacloy, are tasked to clear an abandoned van. I'm told afterwards that the imprint of six milk churns was apparent on the floor of the van.

Was this PIRA's response to our earlier success? I think it was.

I declare the crater free from explosives and the main recovery begins with the casualties. It's clear that their deaths have been instantaneous. It might seem remarkable, given the damage to the vehicle, but the bodies are recovered almost completely intact. Each of them, held together by their uniform and webbing straps, is carefully lifted into a body bag. It takes a number of people to do this, as their skeletal frames are completely shattered.

The armoured vehicle had disintegrated. The turret section is embedded in the ground approximately 300 metres away from the crater. One of the wheels, which must itself weigh a hundred pounds or so, has been propelled over a quarter of a mile. It takes the rest of the day and all the following night to recover the many vehicle parts scattered over the fields and also the soldiers' weapons and ammunition.

That evening, a service is held at Bessbrook Mill in memory of the men who

Above: CATO and PW take in the size of the pit.

Right: The device had been similar in size to the one we cleared in the same lane three months earlier.

Below: The turret section was thrown 300 metres.

died. The hall is packed with just about everyone not on duty. All want to pay their respects to their fallen comrades. Each person knows it could just have easily been him. Soldiers reflect society today and few are religious but, at times like this, the church is indispensable in bringing people together to mourn.

The Mill was in a sombre mood for some time afterwards, but the security work went on unabated – as it always does. PIRA must know as well as us that an incident like this only serves to increase the army's resolve to defeat the people responsible.

This was the last serious incident I attended. The following week my replacement arrived to take over the section.

Left: The soldiers' weapons were completely destroyed.

Below: This was the largest section that remained of the armoured vehicle. One wheel was thrown a quarter of a mile.

21ST MAY 1981

Handover

I know my replacement well; we served in the same unit in Germany and attended courses together. As part of the handover we attend an incident together and he leads in the recovery of a number of American bolt action rifles. These weapons have been used to provide a salute at the funeral of a PIRA member. The rifles were spotted by an army covert observation post as they were being spirited away to a hide after the funeral. The recovery from beneath a hedge is straightforward and uneventful.

The remaining handover formalities are carried out to schedule. Weapons, ammunition, explosives and classified documents are checked, accounted for and then signed off. We discuss some of the incidents the team have dealt with and I introduce him to the people he'll be working with.

My time at Bessbrook is ended. The four months have flashed past. The team and I have dealt with forty-one incidents in total. Most involved terrorist explosives. Those that had detonators in place are classed as live devices and we had neutralised seven; the largest of which was the Chancellors Road culvert device with its booby trapped firing point. Easily the most complex incident had been the radio controlled attack on the police station at Warrenpoint (which had caused me so much grief with the SATO). The mortar attack at Newtownhamilton was a set piece, well coordinated by PIRA and typical of their modus operandi to kill and gain publicity for it. But, by the grace of God and through mainly the efforts of the Royal Engineers, they were thwarted in both. At the second Chancellors Road incident, PIRA eventually got the success they were so desperate for, and in a big way. The other devices – the beer keg on the railway line, the blast incendiaries, the ambush devices at the H25 border crossing and the under-car booby traps – were the flotsam and jetsam of an interminable battle of wills that, at that time, had no end in sight.

Overall, my tour was a microcosm of the tragedy which is Ulster, written as it is in the shattered lives of the families and friends of those left behind on all sides.

I feel some regret at leaving it all behind. Just at the point, I guess, when I've gained the maximum experience. Having said that, I'm also aware that an operator can have a shelf life. Without necessarily realising it yourself, there are patterns to the way you work, which can and will be exploited by the enemy. Four months is enough.

The new ATO, Mick O'Neill, is an experienced warrant officer and, as a second tour operator, knows what he has to do. He will have his own ways of working. Hopefully, he will have a better relationship with the SATO than I had.

25TH MAY 1981

Endex

At my final interview with the SATO, he presents me with my end of tour report. The grading is mediocre, but his comments are frankly better than I expected coming from him. His report very much contradicts much of what he said to me immediately following the Warrenpoint job. I'm somewhat wrong-footed by this.

In the second section of the report, I note that the CATO has endorsed the SATO's comments, but has up-rated the grading. He is also kind enough to state that I've been a credit to the corps.

I'm uncomfortable in the SATO's presence. I don't have much to say to him. Any matters I might have raised go unsaid. To be honest, I'm just glad to get out of the place intact and, for most of us I think, that is enough.

I fly out of the province on Monday 25th May 1981.

Back at Didcot, on leave, I pay my respects to one of the soldiers killed in the Chancellors Road explosion. I attend his funeral in Abingdon. I never knew the lad, but there is an affinity between all those who serve operationally, which is never more apparent than on occasions such as these. I read in the local newspaper that his father is convinced that they will be burying a coffin full of rocks; that the lad was blown to bits. I wish I could have assured him that it wasn't the case.

At the end of the ceremony the firing party fires a volley of shots; the Last Post is sounded; the final prayers are said and everyone disperses; the devastated family members are left to try and comfort each other. It's just one event of many. A small measure of the misery that has been brought to thousands of family members and friends since the troubles commenced. But the cost in these terms is not the key factor and it never will be. Individuals are always sacrificed for principles. Everyone on all sides will keep at it until the politicians can settle it. Whatever the cost, the principles are the overriding factor. It's easy to say and promote, I guess, until you lose someone close.

31ST MAY 1981

A Further Tragedy

Six days after leaving the Province, I'm still on leave with my wife and children and doing the family rounds. On the morning of Sunday 31st May we drive from my mother's house in Poulton-le-Fylde across the Pennines to my wife's parents in Halifax. As I enter their house, my father-in-law comments that the

BBC are reporting that a soldier has been killed in Newry. I reply that, since the army has just pulled out of Newry and the police have taken over patrolling there, I find this surprising. Suddenly, I have a bad feeling and I say as much to my wife.

At 1 p.m. the news comes on the radio again. The soldier killed that morning is named. It's my replacement Mick O'Neill. The shock is jaw dropping. I'm stunned. Anyone who's been thumped in the stomach will know the feeling. I step back and sit down heavily. My wife bursts into tears. I can only imagine what it must be like for his wife and kids, what they're going through.

That afternoon, I telephone the Bessbrook Section. The guys are downbeat, in shock. I speak with the No. 2, Barny. He tells me the team had been tasked to clear a car abandoned at a road junction near Newry. The car had been re-plated and re-sprayed (i.e. twinned) and then used in the murder of a police officer outside a pub at Whitecross. An anonymous telephone call to the police shortly afterwards reported the car's whereabouts and that they had seen armed men getting out of it.

The team deployed at first light. Given the seriousness of the incident, the ATO had gone easy on the car, presumably to preserve any forensic evidence that might be available. Following a series of manual approaches, nothing untoward had been discovered. The clearance was nearing completion. Exactly what happened next is unclear. Whilst the No. 2 was in the back of the team Transit getting equipment together, an explosion occurred that blew the car to bits. No one had been watching the car at the time so, at first, no one knew what had happened. Then it quickly became clear that the ATO was missing. The No. 2 searched for and found the body. He took control of the incident and preserved the scene until the SATO arrived. As the lad had only been in theatre a fortnight himself, I think he did well.

The SATO completed the remainder of the investigation. His report reads that, in all likelihood, it was either a pressure-type switch in a seat or, more likely, something in the glove compartment. Tests were subsequently carried out on similar cars, but the type of device that killed Mick O'Neill was never confirmed.

The SATO's technical appreciation of the tragedy was professional, but his tendency to lash out surfaced once again. The No. 2 got it in the neck because he wasn't watching the ATO at the time he was killed; even though it was the ATO who had returned to the vehicle without telling anyone. The lad was gutted by the criticism. Suffice it to say that there are some officers that soldiers are happier to go to the wire with – and then there are the others.

I don't know if that IED on the 31st May 1981 had my name on it. I ask myself if I would have tackled it differently and don't like the answer I keep coming up with. We all realised the importance of forensic evidence and I had my own policy of bringing things back in one piece.

Mick O'Neill was, in my humble opinion, a gallant and brave man. This task, however, was made more dangerous because he was trying to help solve the murder of an off-duty police officer. Unbeknown to him, the device had been designed to get him; PIRA knew that, in these circumstances, he would feel obliged to take risks.

I didn't attend his funeral. By then it had all got to be too much. I couldn't stomach another funeral – any more tragedies. His death came as I was also trying to find time to grieve for the loss of my father. During my tour I had striven to put all thoughts of him completely out of my mind. Looking back, I also realise that I was shocked at how close I had come to being killed. Into this mix was the bitterness and anger I felt for the SATO, who had so nearly ruined my career. I churned inside with anger. It took years before all that negativity eased its way out of my system and I could at least talk about it without throwing a track. Nonetheless, undoubtedly, I retain some of the scars today.

LAST LIGHT

If commanding that unique unit was a stressful business then, in his case, the SATO certainly liked to spread it about. My team and I were unsettled by his aggressive and unreasoning attitude and this impaired my judgement on at least one occasion. There was something about me that rankled him and it affected every aspect of our relationship. In IEDD, the strains of the job are enough without that kind of distraction. Those of us who experienced it had a right to expect more.

I don't doubt that the SATO was held in high esteem by his superiors and he went on to climb the slippery career pole and, in due course, achieved the rank of full colonel. He didn't, however, receive an award for his tour of duty during 1981, but was eventually awarded the OBE for something different. I never met the guy again – why would I want to? – except, perhaps, to rewrite his end of tour report.

The CATO, however, will be listed in most soldiers' minds as a 'good bloke', as indeed the vast majority of senior officers are in my experience. He was well respected by those who served under him and I was very glad to have had his support. Perhaps the strength of having two senior appointments preside over 321 EOD Company was that one might be a moderating influence over the other when it became necessary.

The CATO received the OBE for his tour and I expect he went on to greater things. I was glad to meet up with him again when he was the commanding officer of the Army School of Ammunition at Kineton in Warwickshire.

The mediocre grade of my end of tour report didn't hold me back for long. A couple of years later, I was promoted to warrant officer class 1. Not long after that, I was selected by the corps to be a 'conductor'. This is an ancient and honourable appointment, little publicised, which is conferred on only a few RAOC warrant officers class 1 at a time. This small, select band are considered the most senior warrant officers in the British Army. This is an assertion that always makes for good arguments at regimental dinners.

CLEAR DOWN

Working to mandatory procedures in Northern Ireland proved to be the safest way of approaching IEDs; this was brought forward from the structured working practices and methods required for servicing and disposing of ammunition. Such techniques worked pretty well. At times, however, it barely took into account the reality of working at the coal face. For example, it wasn't always possible, practical or feasible to refer up to a senior officer as and when the procedure required it and when you didn't you left yourself open to criticism. Alternatively, at the other end of the spectrum, applying all the secondary waiting periods according to the book was often completely impractical. Accordingly, many reports were written according to how the job should have been dealt with rather than how the operator actually went about it.

Our Render Safe Procedures were developed and quickly redeveloped in response to operator deaths early in the campaign. They became a catch-all to cover all circumstances but, because the techniques weren't viewed as a framework or a tool box, they often became a bureaucracy. As a bureaucracy, they were often overseen in a rigid way. It was almost impossible then to function properly without contravening the rules in one way or another. The rules, therefore, became something to beat you with if someone was of a mind to. Furthermore, despite the rigidity, there was a rule for one if not for the others. CATOs and SATOs were pretty much a law unto themselves and worked the RSPs in their own way. I think many of them would accept this.

For the more experienced operators, I think greater flexibility in the application of the RSPs should have been allowed. It was getting the balance right that we can argue about. I guess, if everyone behaved like Staff Sgt IM from 3 BAPD you could understand it, but, fortunately, Staff Sgt IM was very much the exception. Nonetheless, it sometimes felt like an assumption had been made that we would behave like SSgt IM if we were not reigned in.

Many military leaders will appreciate, from experience, that plans tend to go out of the window on first contact with the enemy. Similarly, IEDD situations could and would change from moment to moment and, when they did, you had to cope with the situation as it evolved around you as best you could. The other agencies involved always had to be considered, whatever the teaching at pre-ops courses, and time is always a factor. Yes, your actions may incur additional risk to you; you do your best to reduce them, but these risks go with the job. But the people you're supporting need to have confidence in you, know that you have the wherewithal to deal with the situation and that you recognise the pressures they are under too. If you're sensible and they're comfortable with you then you are probably doing OK. When they aren't, and it can happen, because IEDD clearance operations can still take an awful long time, the operator needs the backing of the powers that be to support his decisions. Before this problem was recognised, operators could find themselves under pressure to take action quicker than would otherwise be acceptable today.

An operator, therefore, walked a tightrope; discrepancies between what the book says and what he felt was appropriate at any given time could be interpreted as stepping out of line and this, in turn, could be viewed as recklessness. The upshot of all this is that, by expecting operators to toe the procedural line precisely, any error they make is seen as a contravention. This thinking, I believe, had a bearing on how their deaths were perceived in some quarters.

RECOGNITION

Awards have become an integral part of this work. This subject was the catalyst that prompted the SATO to speak with me at the NI pre-ops course. Clearly, he had a bee in his bonnet about it. So it was a surprise to me when, on 14th December 1981, it was published in the London Gazette that I had been Mentioned in Despatches (MID) for gallantry. I was grateful to have been recognised in this way when many colleagues weren't. Among others, I received a congratulatory letter from the CATO and also letters from the commanding officers of the two infantry regiments I served with.

It's not hard to see why 321 EOD Company became the most decorated unit in the history of the British Army when its men were prepared to walk into the jaws of death and spit in the devil's eye time and time again. In the annals that will undoubtedly be written, as it is throughout history, it will tend to be those who received the highest honours who are most likely to be remembered first.

So, like many things people covet, medals and awards can be a driving influence because, let's face it, there is much kudos in being awarded one. Society uses this as a measure for who they think has been brave and gallant. It is a tenuous measure I'm afraid – or, at the very least, it only tells part of the story.

Some myths about my own profession need exploding here. A study carried out in 1981 by the University of London into fearlessness and courage tried to show that there are physiological differences between operators who received awards and those who did not. This type of thinking is completely irrational because, actually, most guys I know will deal effectively with whatever is put in front of them. What shit does come their way is random, because it's down to enemy tactics. Notwithstanding some really heroic acts, whether an ATO is awarded a medal afterwards is subject to a number of variables. For example, it can depend on the weight of IEDD activity at a given point in time. That is, one incident can seem big and important in isolation, but could be seen as routine during high activity. Some people don't get put up for awards for many reasons; some receive lesser awards and some are rejected. The intensity of the Northern Ireland bombing campaign was such that many others could also have won awards if their circumstances had been reported upon differently. Some remarkable acts of courage by ATOs were instead punished – seen as reckless. For example, I know of one staff sergeant who neutralised two devices placed in derelicts, timed to function as a Protestant march passed by. Because diverting marches can be problematic, he walked up and disrupted each device in turn and this allowed the march to pass by uninterrupted. He thought it the right thing to do. But, instead of echoing the praise of the troops on the ground, our people nearly crucified him. There will be many other stories like this. The awarding of gallantry medals is hit and miss and some deserving individuals are unfortunately missed.

So, my own profession, and also those looking into it, shouldn't get too carried away believing we have a meaningful way of measuring who contributed most. It is not a cast iron way of quantifying bravery. Group photographs and engraved plaques that reflect award winners, in my opinion, mainly serve to ignore and undervalue the very many other unsung foot soldiers of this profession who stepped into the dragon's den time and again, but didn't receive recognition for it. You might say this type of problem exists everywhere else too. Well OK, but I maintain that it is much more obvious here.

A SYSTEM FAILURE?

Did our dead deserve formal recognition? Well, yes, I think many did. The early years of the Irish Campaign were the formative years when most of our losses occurred. It was at a time when the thinking around explosive devices and making them safe still had to be cemented. Our equipment was in its infancy. People felt under pressure to get jobs done quickly. It was also the first time the profession had been pitted against a Western terrorist organisation who could call upon first world technology in the manufacture of their devices; at least one bomb maker during this period came to the party with an electrical engineering background.

The tactical options open to the enemy are always many and varied, but bomb disposal operators are not blessed with either hindsight or second sight. Instead, on what is often minimal information, they have to make a rapid assessment and then get on with it. In the heat of the moment, it is too easy to come to a wrong conclusion. But then it was the operator alone who entered the dragon's den and if the dragon roared its white-hot breath it was he alone who died – not someone else. I may be accused of being a partisan here, but if that is not an act of gallantry I do not know what is.

For much of the early NI campaign, the enemy revised their methods and our techniques had to be redeveloped accordingly. Sometimes, however, we were behind their innovations. Because of this, an NI operator worked not only in a highly hazardous and unpredictable set of circumstances, but it was also a novel experience because everything was so immature and dynamic. I expect too that it was an especially frightening experience, not having the disruptive equipment and remote capability that were developed later.

By 1973, ten operators had been killed. It was an attrition rate that the profession could not have sustained for any length of time and the development of more effective Render Safe Procedures went on concurrently, consistently and at a pace.

As I have come to appreciate even more from writing this book, there were weaknesses in my own questioning technique, misunderstandings and underestimations of the threats. Operators faced each dangerous situation according to an assessment, which hinged on speech, hearing and comprehension. In a tense, fast-moving situation what seemed to be the truth of it could easily be flawed. The sheer quantity of incidents that had to be dealt with in the early days, especially in the two cities, Belfast and Londonderry, might also be factored in. Operators could have tasks stacked up and would have to categorise them into an order of priority. In one four-month tour, an operator could be called upon to deal with well over 100 incidents. On each of those separate occasions, this ordinary guy, with a nominal amount of training, entered a dragon's den voluntarily on behalf of Queen and Country and, at that point, his family and friends were left behind – not once, but every time.

When we were transitioning from the passive to the offensive strategies, operators were expected to sandbag a device in order to reduce the likelihood of collateral damage, since the thinking was that the brick walls of a shop were worth endangering these men's lives for. For those who died, who felt the full force of the dragon's breath, it was the very act of walking into the dragon's den that was, in my opinion, the gallant act.

In the Northern Ireland conflict, the medals awarded for this work were pretty much based on hypotheticals. For example, the device might have gone off, or it might have caused X amount of damage. Citations were written up on how long a clearance took or how many manual approaches were necessary. Fair enough, but, hey, many devices for which people received top awards would probably never have gone off at all; some of mine too. Of course, this is after the fact and I don't want to decry many whose awards were well deserved. But there can be no argument as to which devices were the most dangerous; they were those that killed our colleagues. There can be no question as to who sacrificed more; it was their wives and their families. There can be no question as to who was let down; it was them.

How should we measure the work? Well, first and foremost, I think the public do get value for money from Ammunition Technicians and the value is in having people who are prepared to get qualified and willing to step into these dragon's dens on behalf of our country. It's not the salary is it? No one was, or is, paid anything extra for doing this job. For the families, it is to be hoped that the new, and very welcome, Queen Elizabeth Medal, which is awarded to the families of all service personnel killed on active service, will provide them an opportunity to recount and relate the contributions of their loved ones.

For Ammo Techs, I still think that the unique nature of those sacrifices during this campaign, for the reasons I have covered in this book, but also for posterity, are worthy of some form of collective recognition.

Why weren't our people recognised individually? Well, this appears to have been a policy matter. Up until the Falklands War, the MoD, apparently, did not allow gallantry medals to be awarded posthumously (except for the VC, GC or Mentioned in Despatches. These are class 1 and class 4 awards; no class 2 or 3 awards). It is impossible to comprehend the logic of this policy now. It was clearly bonkers, because the anomaly was, in fact, rectified around 1979. When it came to applying for an award, the class 1 may have been considered too high and then the MID might have been considered too low. Of course, this does not account for why the two operators killed after this date also missed out.

This medals policy was contrary to the policy of other services like, for example, the police force. In one way, it is a relief to find that it was a form of MoD bureaucracy and not my hierarchy or profession that had fallen down on the job. It's a pity there was no Joanna Lumley to fight the case back then.

A consequence of this flawed medals policy is that many of us thought that those killed had been found by our own people to be partly culpable for their own deaths – that the lack of any award was to encourage adherence to procedures. This thinking was occasionally visible in our training. Many of us regret that now.

Whilst I have argued that oversight of the Render Safe Procedures could sometimes be too rigid, it was important to have them and, for this, we have those who didn't return from the long walk to thank. New techniques were introduced or modified as a direct result of the lessons learned from those tragedies. It was those guys who were the pathfinders in this business and, in my opinion, the real heroes – every single one of them. No one on our side is to blame for the deaths of our operators, least of all themselves – it was the war.

Some people had a strange view that operators came to the job with something like a death wish: a willingness to risk all for the glory. I don't think so. I think most people just wanted to do a good job and get home. Doing a 'good job' would, in my opinion, be measured in terms of meeting the needs and expectations of the populace and other agencies involved. That's the reality and, in the real world, it required additional risks to be taken. These are personal risks taken with the best of intentions. Men who took those risks need not have been crucified for that.

By 1982 I am still serving with Proof Branch at Didcot and, in that summer, I am seconded to the MoD Defence Sales Organisation for a project called Floater '83. The MoD has commissioned the Townsend Thoreson roll-on, roll-off channel ferry, Viking Venturer, for a tour of the Middle East the following year.

As an aside, this is the sister ship to the Herald of Free Enterprise: the ship that capsized in March 1987 at Zeebrugge when the bow door was left open after departure. The sea flooded the car decks leading to the death of 190 people.

Our ship was to be converted to a floating exhibition and the defence industries invited to participate and show off their wares; that is everything from tanks and missiles, to uniforms and carbide batteries. Fire power displays would take place and for this they would need a lot of ammunition. Hence, they would need, what is called, an Authorised Representative to fulfil the Department of Trade ammunition and Explosive regulations, i.e. me.

The DoT would normally allow only 10 kg of high explosive to be transported on a passenger ship and so my first job is to design an explosive magazine that can hold 30 tons of ammunition and explosives and then get the Department of Trade to issue an exemption certificate that will allow it to be used. This I duly do – no problem encountered at this stage.

I report for the tour in January as the ship is due to depart from Southampton in a blaze of media glory. Unfortunately, it doesn't happen like that.

The ship should have been fitted out in France, but it arrives in Southampton only partially completed – a week behind schedule, due to French union trouble. The media fest is, therefore, cancelled.

I don't have an axe to grind in terms of unions and, in many ways, they fulfil a useful service, but union trouble became a common theme in this project. When it became time to load all the military vehicles and equipment onto the ship the union(s) wouldn't allow it until additional payments were made. These were refused. The standoff continued into the early hours of the night. And, in case the military dispensed with the diplomatic niceties and decided to load the ship themselves, the union parked a fork-lift truck across the ship's drawbridge to block the access.

The message comes through the grapevine. 'Stand to, all drivers'. The ship would complete its loading at the union free military port of Marchwood.

If anyone in Southampton had looked out at 3 a.m. in the morning,

...ey will have seen a convoy of about thirty sand-coloured vehicles that included two main battle tanks and other tracked vehicles under police escort steaming through their streets. In case anyone did and thought they were being invaded, well, they weren't – the military had just invented a cunning plan to escape what everyone felt was union bloodymindedness!

The ship slips its moorings and crosses the Solent to Marchwood. Throughout the night, loading continues apace and, eventually, the ammunition is hoisted onboard to be stacked into the configuration I have designed for it. The work is completed the following mid-morning and the ship sets sail a little later than originally anticipated.

Onboard are a bevy of painters, joiners and electricians working to complete the unfinished exhibition stands. They depart the ship at Gibraltar. The tour has not got off to the best start.

The next day we are into the teeth of a storm as the ship passes through the Bay of Biscay. I am not normally seasick, but just about everyone else is and breakfast is, therefore, a lonely event.

What I know or care about ships you could fit on a sixpence. I also know very little about the forces they are subjected to. If I'd wanted to know all this, I guess I'd have joined the Navy. Anyway, I was about to learn it the hard way.

As the ship powers its way through the tempestuous seas, great waves crash over the forward decks where two large ISO containers have been positioned. These hold the ammunition that should not be stored below decks. It occurs to me that I would be showing due diligence if I checked out this ammunition to ensure it wasn't being damaged in any way. I suppose the only other reason I can give is that it seemed to make good sense at the time!

Venturing out on deck was going to be somewhat risky, given the heaving decks, so I told my friend, Tony Harveson, of my intentions and he said he'd keep a weather eye on me and the situation. Tony was a member of the army Small Arms School Corps and the guy with whom I was sharing a bunk.

I shuffle across the deck hanging onto anything that looks immovable and finally arrive at the two large ISO containers. I unhook one of the large door stays just as a wave breaks over the deck and soaks me to the skin. Undeterred, I open the door slightly to look inside. At that moment the ship, riding an even larger wave, rears right up, causing the wall of loose ammunition boxes inside (about 2 tons in weight) to shift towards me, just enough to prevent me from closing the door. Now I am stuck. I can't close the door, can't leave and every time the ship rears up the wall of boxes shifts again slightly, pushing the door open ever wider. There is a grave danger that the ammunition will spill out onto the decks and be washed overboard – and me if I lose my grip!

Any pressure I can apply to get the boxes back in position is futile and the situation is becoming unrecoverable with every big wave. As disaster stares me in the face, Tony Harveson appears at my side. Above the sound of waves crashing around us, I am able to yell into his ear my predicament. As I hang on for grim death, he shoots off and returns with some hefty blokes to help hold the doors together. Even so, this can only be a delaying tactic rather than a solution.

At this point, the merchant navy get involved when we are spotted from the Bridge. A window is flung open and a very irate first officer gives me what was almost certainly an ear-bashing and perhaps even some advice, but it is all completely drowned out by the roaring seas – even the expletives!

A short time later though, a guy from the engine room appears with a thick metal chain and we wrap this around the door stays. It prevents the two doors from coming apart. They are somewhat ajar, however, but not enough to allow the ammunition packages to fall out. The situation is saved and the ship is able to plough on through the remainder of the storm without further ado.

On arriving at Gibraltar, I restack the container and relock it. After this escapade, the ship's captain dubs me the 'mad bomber'. Fortunately, there were no more ammunition-related mishaps during the two-month tour and I like to think I regained everyone's respect as the tour progressed.

Both parties learned something from this episode: I learn that there is a bit more to this sailoring lark than I had realised and the Merchant Navy learned that they are going to have their hands full dealing with a hundred or so landlubbers who are completely oblivious to the rules of engagement onboard ships!

Getting an understanding of ship-type protocol and amendments to the chain of command are just some of the learnings that occupy the army during the early days of the tour.

Communications are always important (no less here) and are problematic throughout the trip. It begins as we approach Gibraltar. The CO, seeing an opportunity to raise the profile of the tour, orders the Scots Guards piper into his full regalia and from the foc'sle to play the ship into port. Unfortunately, the ship lumbers into an oil bunkering terminal and so Jock's best efforts to impress are pretty much wasted. I'm sure the few dockers who turn out wondering what the noise is all about enjoy it, though. As for Jock, he drowns his embarrassment with a few pints in the bar afterwards, so he's alright. Nonetheless the inauspicious start to the tour has not been diminished by this little event.

A variety of military demonstration teams travel with the ship, but the 100 plus civilian salesmen don't. They fly from port to port, so I don't see too much of them.

Overall, I don't know if the tour is ultimately a success, if it should be measured in terms of additional business for the participating defence industries.

Commissioned by the Defence Sales Organisation for Floater 83, MV *Viking Venturer* at port in one of the Gulf States with our military vehicles displayed on the quayside. An open bow door would cause its sister ship to capsize at Zeebrugge a few years later.

Such matters aren't discussed. I suspect that it isn't, given the political situation at this time and the difficulties we encounter with the various authorities. We aren't even allowed off the ship at Damman in Saudi Arabia.

In Bahrain, I meet up with John Woodward, an ex-warrant officer Ammo Tech who, with his wife, Jackie, lives there as an ex-patriot. John provides an IEDD capability for the police. Then, in Dubai, I meet John Sheldrake and his wife Rita – another ex-Ammo Tech warrant officer providing a similar service to the police. John Sheldrake later offered me a job and, I have to say, I was tempted by the money but, in the end, it seemed too big a step for my family and I don't think I would ever have felt secure there. There was then, and there probably still is today, a great demand for Ammo Tech skills across the globe since the world hasn't got any safer.

Back on the tour, the defence industry salesmen are highly competitive and it is funny watching the two sets of main battle tank (MBT) teams, for example, competing for favours; insisting that their tank isn't getting the same exposure/treatment as the other. But, on the range in Bahrain, both those tanks are out-gunned by a young army gunner in a light Scorpion vehicle who, with his obsolescent 76 mm gun, manages to hit a moving target at a range that is way off the gun sight scale! This gets a hefty cheer from all the spectators.

May 1983, at the end of the Defence Sales tour. Presenting the Ship's Master, Captain Robin Plant, with the RAOC plaque.

On this tour, I do get to fire a silenced, fully chromed sub-machine gun, which is quite an experience. The only sound is the firing pin block clunking the face of the breech. I also get to fire a 40 mm anti-riot gun manufactured by Enfield – the ARWEN. The gun has a repeat firing capability and an imaginative range of baton-type rounds. This is too effective, though, to be acceptable for use in the UK, since it would obviously be an infringement of people's civil rights to respond to bricks and stones with an effective anti-riot tool.

I learn a lot from this tour. For example:

• Driving in convoy at night on a dual carriageway through Egypt is not like driving in most other places. Cars come straight at us, on our side of the road, and without headlights!

• Soldiers need to be protected. For example, the British Army beret is no defence against the swirling dust clouds of a Kuwaiti hubbub. The problem hasn't been anticipated. The fine grit gets behind your eyes, blinds you, fills up your nose and it can bury large objects left on the ground within minutes.

• Forget the endless romantic-looking sand dunes of the Lawrence of Arabia film. In Kuwait, it is just an endless and barren wilderness of grey dust and unforgiving rock or, as the troops call it, MAMFA, i.e. Miles and Miles of F*ck All.

• Range safety isn't all it could be in the Gulf states. After a fire power demonstration, where all our big guns have been blazing away doing their stuff, we find out that Kuwaiti forces have been encamped in the impact area!

• The Ship's Master is to be respected, especially when (in order to meet the schedule) he makes a personal and potentially career-busting decision to leave the port at Dubai into the teeth of a storm. As we leave the harbour entrance, the rising and falling sea levels could easily have broken the back of the ship.

• Adapt to the culture as you find it. Many carrier bags containing cigarettes and booze smooth the way through the Suez Canal. In addition, large sums are demanded by port authorities just to allow us to unload the vehicles.

• That the Suez Canal is, in fact, a number of joined-up large lakes. The signs of previous wars are everywhere.

• The naval might of the USA is impressive. In the Suez Canal, all ships have to give way to one US aircraft carrier and escort ships. They are clearly geared up for business since the crew has been stood to and their tooled-up helicopters buzz around like demented bees!

• The beauty of the Arabian night and the clarity of the stars. Looking into this abyss with an image intensifier, i.e. rifle night sight, nearly blows my mind. And during the day, the range of life in the Arabian Sea is absolutely fascinating.

• Sunbathing on ships is best done standing up, reading a book.

TRAINING AMMO TECHS

Towards the end of 1983 I'm posted out of Didcot to the Army School of Ammunition as an instructor on IEDD Branch. By now the school had transferred from Bramley to the Ammunition Depot at Kineton in Warwickshire. I take over from my friend, George Ferguson.

The courses are geared up to train and test our own people, of course, but also explosive experts from many countries across the globe. These are comprehensive and, ultimately, exacting courses – usually a week of theory, a week of syndicate practices and then practical exams in a simulated operational setting. The training hasn't much changed from the mid-seventies except that various levels have been introduced: basic, intermediate and advanced, and then there are the specific pre-operational courses.

Seeing the training from the inside doesn't change my view of how difficult it is, in 1983, to qualify as an IEDD Operator – and for all the wrong reasons. As I say, you have to be able to imagine the setting, interpret the risks at this imaginary scene and then consider every possible threat. Some have said that playing that game is often tougher than the real thing!

To be honest, I don't enjoy the job very much. Everyone at the branch seems to be at each other's throats most of the time and one-upmanship is rife. Perhaps Myers-Briggs could have helped us here! Some colleagues have a kind of macho and self-inflated view of themselves, which comes across as somewhat elitist. It must come with the job because, over the years, this has often been commented upon by those on the outside. Now, being part of it, I see how it arises.

This faintly bizarre culture is not helped by the then OC, Major NG, whose unsympathetic and overbearing manner would often wind up even his most trusted sycophants.

To be fair on the branch, it is under a lot of pressure both in the number of courses it has to run and the need to get people qualified, whilst at the same time maintaining minimum standards. Despite its obvious importance, it is just one of those jobs that you know instinctively isn't for you. When a vacancy arises in the Conventional Land Ammunition Branch, I apply for it and get it.

CLA Branch has a significantly different culture; it is just as committed to its work, but is much more relaxed in the approach. I teach the practice and theory of ammunition surveillance, proof and repair: subjects that are more in keeping with my service history and closer to where my aspirations lie within the profession. I am, after all, an Ammunition Technician not a bomb disposal operator.

Wharton instructing potential Ammo Techs in the various inspection points on an HE artillery shell.

In 1984, I'm promoted to Warrant Officer Class 1 and ask for (and am given) the appointment of Senior Ammunition Technician within the Ammunition Depot here at Kineton. As the SAT, I oversee twelve ammunition process buildings, a proof centre and a demolition ground. I also have responsibility for maintaining the technical standards of over 60 Ammunition Technicians of all ranks.

Coming from the school, and therefore the centre of competence for all things ammunition, I am dismayed by what I have already seen as poor working practices. I, therefore, have it on my mind to drive more stringent standards into the ammunition process area.

Coincidently, as I take up the appointment, my opinion is pretty much proven when we are notified by Didcot that a socket spanner has been discovered, by the user, in a Javelin Dart practice missile immediately prior to it being fired. This must have been left inside during its conversion for training purposes. Fortunately, no one is injured this time. Our investigation reveals that a toxic mix of throughput (i.e. quantity rather than quality, together with poor oversight) had created the situation where such a problem could arise. It would have been too easy to simply blame the young Ammunition Technician responsible, but I wanted the underlying problems taken seriously. He, more or less, got off with it and I have a mandate to get a grip of the place.

By the time I leave the job in 1986, I like to think I've made a mark. As far as I'm concerned, the SAT job there is one of the most important in the trade. Again, no one can afford to take their eye off the ball; dangers are always there lurking in left field.

In 1985, I'm nominated for another shift in the paradigms of life; my turn has come for a six-month tour of duty in the Falkland Islands.

FALKLAND ISLANDS AMMUNITION INSPECTORATE — 1985

In 1982, the Falkland Islands are recaptured from the Argentinians and the Islands duly drop out of the worldwide media show. The fighting Brigade is replaced by a Logistics Battalion and a Garrison to defend it in the unlikely event that the Argentinians come back for another lesson in soldiering.

Shortly afterwards, an Ammunition Inspectorate is established, commanded by a major. In 1985, as a warrant officer class 1, I am deployed to the unit as the islands' Senior Ammunition Technician.

The clear up is just about complete by the time I arrive and the new multi-million pound Mount Pleasant airport is in use but still a busy building site. MPA would make the islands easier to reinforce, since the airport at the capital, Stanley, is only good for small aircraft.

MPA has been located in the remote centre of the main island, making it easier to defend, and a road has, therefore, been laid all the way back to Stanley, some 20-plus miles away. At this time, MPA is a manic place with up to 5000 contractors working 24/7 on a variety of construction projects.

I arrive after a long British Airways flight, together with about 200 others. It is teeming with rain. We are immediately loaded onto a series of military buses and conveyed to Stanley. I am told that the long road to Stanley is a major engineering feat in itself. Imagining the terrain, it isn't hard to see why. When I say it is a road, however, I have probably overstated it. It is actually a wide, rough, rocky track, pock-marked with deep, muddy holes. The buses are ill-suited to negotiate this type of terrain and the long journey is, therefore, slow, bumpy and tedious to say the least.

I see nothing of the island during the ninety-minute bus journey from MPA; the windows are coated in a thick layer of impenetrable mud! It is like travelling through a long, dark, bumpy tunnel. The rain beating on the windows, however, is a constant reminder of where we are.

At Stanley, I'm met by the guy I'm replacing, Jerry Lewis, and spirited off to the Ammo Inspectorate offices, i.e. a portakabin.

Soldiers based around Stanley mainly live on three coastels. These are large floating accommodation centres, which have been loaned from the oil industry. Each could house up to 800 troops. Inside the enclosed area, each floor has a long corridor with alcoves containing bunks and ablutions. I live in an alcove with other warrant officers of various cap badges. We called the alcove 'Dear Hunters', because any old dear will do! Clever eh? Alright, please yourself!

Except for duty personnel, soldiers work a six-day week and I often spend the seventh roaming the former battlefields around Stanley. Each one of those aptly named hills, where the fighting was some of the fiercest, has its own story to tell. Such stories are now well documented. For example, Mount Harriet was captured by the Royal Marines and Mount Tumbledown by the Scots Guards. Then there is Mount Longdon with the approach to it still blocked, to date, by a large minefield that 3 Para had to skirmish through during the night attack.

On Tumbledown, I come across the Argentinian command bunker with its myriad of telephone cables running in all directions. Everywhere, there are signs of war – craters, Argentinean equipment and clothing scattered around; most of it is burned.

On each of those hills is a memorial to our glorious dead.

It isn't easy now, all these years afterwards, to appreciate what our troops went through to defeat the enemy on those bleak, craggy, but gentle slopes. Maybe, however, it's too easy to forget it.

In the darkness, men would hear conflicting commands; the confusion would have been great: the crackle of machine guns with the tracer rounds passing left

Above: Stanley from Tumbledown. Moody Brook RM Barracks is on the left of the bay and the Canache area is at the very top of the picture.

Left : With my back to the Argentinean Command Bunker on Mount Tumbledown. Circa July 1985.

and right; the crack and thump of the rifle round; the thump, thump of mortars and artillery shells that did not always single out the enemy; dead bodies in grotesque poses. There must have been great fear, terrific noise, and the screams of the wounded from both sides would have echoed around the rocks in those sporadic bursts of silence. As illumination flares burned out, scary blindness would follow until your eyes re-adjusted what would seem a lifetime later.

The battles often amounted to actions by small groups of men, isolated from the rest by the darkness. They took on the foe they could sense in front of them, not knowing how many they were up against. Great acts of leadership and gallantry will almost certainly have gone unrecognised.

Young men killed others with their bayonets for the first and only time in their lives, never to fully recover from the experience. In this fog of war, people were mistakenly shot by their own side and some will take these secrets to the grave. After these experiences, many soldiers would leave the army at the first opportunity.

It might not have been easy to appreciate what it had been like on those few nights in 1982, but I tried my best.

In 1985 there are still over 100 minefields around Stanley. Each had been identified, surveyed and fenced off by the Royal Engineers; a number of whom had been injured carrying out this work in the early days. The areas were mainly contaminated with plastic, undetectable mines the size of a shoe polish tin, which the Argentinians had scattered in front of their positions. Stand on one and you would lose a leg, as a minimum. The Royal Engineers' job in 1985 is to manage these fields and maintain the fences and we had a good working relationship with those guys during my time there.

On one Sunday excursion with another Ammo Tech, Tony Thorogood, we come across what must have been the British artillery position for the final attack on Stanley. At least a thousand brown ammunition containers remain where they had been dumped on the night of the attack. You could easily imagine the gunners extracting and stacking the ammunition prior to the attack.

Also scattered around the area are many live Point Detonating, i.e. impact fuzes, which had been extracted from the shells together with their TNT exploders and also discarded by the gunners in favour of the longer proximity fuzes.

A proximity fuze emits a radar wave and, at the appropriate height (say, 20 ft off the ground), the fuze detonates the shell. When an artillery shell is detonated in this way, thousands of white-hot metal shards are projected in every direction. It is hard to defend yourself against it and woe betide anyone caught out in the open – as the Argentineans were when they retreated into Stanley towards the end of the campaign. It was clear to us, just from looking at the water-filled trenches and boggy ground around, why this method was used.

The following week I had the site cleared up and made safe.

Stories abound of what worked during the conflict and what didn't. For example, the British Army hand grenade was found to be flawed. The Argentineans had to fight from water-filled trenches. When lobbed into one, the water pressure dampened the explosion such that the trench wasn't neutralised. I suspect the White Phosphorous smoke grenade was used to clear trenches instead. Desperate men will use anything to hand.

Many guided weapon systems were used operationally for the first time and were stretched to the limit. None performed as well as might have been expected – except perhaps the RAF sidewinder missile, which came out of it with a 100% hit rate.

Other items of ammunition were deployed in imaginative ways. For example, the wire-guided anti-tank missile, Milan, was used to take out Argentinian gun positions at Goose Green and 66 mm anti-tank rockets were used for the same purpose at Tumbledown. I mean, why wouldn't you?

When I arrived there, British units were still driving Mercedes jeeps. About 100 brand new vehicles had been captured from the Argies, who found out too late that even four wheel drive vehicles were no match for the boggy Falkland terrain. The British prefixed the vehicle plates with CV, meaning 'Captured Vehicle'.

Unfortunately, it came to pass that the Argies had not paid Mercedes for the vehicles. After the war, the bill was sent to the British MoD. They probably said, 'Get stuffed – This is war booty.' Anyway, Mercedes, in a fit of pique, I suppose, had a sense of humour failure over this and wouldn't supply us with any spare vehicle parts.

By 1985, all such vehicles were in a sad shape: cracked windscreens, smashed light covers, and torn and ripped canvas covers, but they were still much-preferred over the more solid British Land Rover, due mainly to the former's power-assisted steering and soft seats! The REME cannibalised the worst vehicles to provide parts for the roadworthy ones. Soon, however, they were all written off. I have very fond memories of CV 64!

The battlefields were still littered with UXBs at this time. Items would be found and reported to us by walkers. It was our job to deal with this stuff, mainly by blowing it up in situ.

Another job I took on was lecturing to the incoming flights at MPA. For me, this meant a long bumpy drive along the very wet or highly dusty road to Mount Pleasant twice a week, so I don't really know why I enjoyed it! People arriving for the first time had to be briefed on the dangers associated with mines and unexploded ammunition. They also had to be reminded that all bags are X-rayed on exit, which was intended to deter souvenir hunting. Examples of Argentinean 'clag' and pictures of hands blown off and worse were used to dissuade people from tampering or getting too close to the minefields. Many minefields, unfortunately, encompassed the lovely white sandy beaches that are dotted around Stanley.

One rather mundane but very key job we had to do for the MoD was recalculating and adjusting the ammunition war reserve stocks to something that matched the types and numbers of units deployed there. Much of the current stock was back-loaded to the UK and new stock shipped out. Disposing of any unserviceable ammunition was becoming a problem at this time as the ecology was being considered more and more. I think we were as careful as we could be.

For us, the Falklands were a non-threatening, semi-operational environment that still hadn't been fully regularised, so there was a refreshing flexibility about the decisions you and others could make.

Entertainment on the islands was pretty minimal – one pub, no cinema and no TV, so the troops found ways to amuse themselves; mainly through parties and functions organised by the various messes. Large quantities of beer helped and so, occasionally, drink-related problems would raise their head – the odd riot would occur, for example.

Fresh fruit arrived only periodically and this was highly prized, so it was worth knowing someone on the catering side. In fact, a lot got done depending on who you knew!

MoD-sponsored Combined Services Entertainment shows arrived at regular intervals and were worth their weight in gold, but, as in Ulster, of all the acts, it was the scantily clad dancing dollies that one tends to remember most fondly!

The six months flashed past. I had a great time as most did. I think it was harder for me to adjust to life in the UK after that tour, than any other. It definitely had attractions that were missed on return to England; there was no crime, no litter, no noise, no television, no reality television, no traffic jams because there was no traffic, and the FI people were still friendly towards us at that time, albeit with gritted teeth (with up to 6,000 strangers to contend with, they were rightly unhappy at the way our tracked vehicles had ploughed up their paths and tracks – damage that was not easy to repair).

It is possible to be seduced by that way of life. Others have commented similarly, but I wonder if it is really nothing more than nostalgia for an era and a culture that has long passed us by here in the UK. How long could most people put up with it? Some might think it's worth a try. A life like that probably only exists today in the far reaches of Scotland – and even there, there is Reality TV!

Have I an opinion on whether the Falklands War was necessary? Who hasn't? Well, having seen it and met the people, I can say it is as much a part of

Great Britain as any other rural island that abound these shores. The distances involved are inconvenient but irrelevant. The Falkland Islanders' way of life has precious little in common with Argentina and to have failed to fight for it would simply have appeased and promoted their aggression – and that of others. Once diplomacy failed, we had no choice. Again, it's the principle.

Above Left: UXB - An Argentinean 105mm Recoiless HE Round found on '12 o Clock mountain'. I've prepared it for demolition.

Above Right: Tony Thorogood, Brian Thomson and I at the Fitzroy settlement with our Haglunds BV. The only vehicle that could easily traverse the islands. The islanders rightly hated them because they churned up the tracks making them impassable for their Land Rovers.

Left: The road to Estancia. One of the few 'roads' in existence prior to the conflict. The captured Mercedes vehicles have their work cut out!

The Coastels - British
military accommodation
at the Canache area near
Stanley. All the roads you
can see were put in by the
army. The hills, where the
majority of the fighting
took place, make an
enigmatic backdrop.

Combined Services
Entertainment. I repeat,
UXBs and IEDs weren't the
only things that got the
heart pounding!

Deep inside the Logistics
Coastel, Warrant Officers of
the 'Dear Hunters' alcove.
The best club in town!

Above: Disposing of unserviceable ammunition on a beach near Stanley. White sands, blue sea, bloody freezing!

Left: Not too many road accidents but this was a gem. The poorly parked Land Rover and the recovery vehicle both ended up in the drink.

Dear Hunters [*sic*] amusing themselves. The fiend waving hello is me. Tony Thorogood is easier to spot with an eyeball in his mouth.

Left: The British low level surface to air Rapier System had some success but was stretched to the limit by the conflict. Maintaining the missiles at standby, 'on the beam', became a logistics exercise.

Suffering in support of Live Aid. One of the hardest things I ever participated in was this Land Rover race up Philomill Hill and then to the Canache area. The Light Infantry beat us, the Logistics Battalion, by a few feet.

In the distance is Mount Longdon. Immediately behind me is the minefield through which the Parachute Regiment had to skirmish on the night of the battle.

Above: The Senior ATO Major DougDoherty with his band of brothers. HQ Ammo Inspectorate, Stanley Airport November 85 'We're right behind you sir!'

Right: The Point Detonating fuzes and TNT exploders are still scattered around three years after the conflict ended.

Destroying a British White Phosphorous Grenade discovered by walkers on the Tumbledown slopes.

An Argy unfuzed mortar bomb. Behind me, the 'gateway' to Stanley.

My second brush with religion occurred in 1987, and when it happened no one was more surprised than me. During a Baptist service in my then home town, Towcester, Northants, I had a Damascus-type conversion experience. We had gone there because we thought that enrolling our children into Sunday School would be a good idea. We did not attend church as a rule. I can only explain the experience as a wave of heat that passed through me with a sudden and dramatic realisation that what I was hearing said about Jesus Christ was all true. The following year, I was baptised in an adult believer's baptism ceremony. Soon after that, too soon I guess, I was elected by the congregation to be a leader in the church, i.e. a deacon. With this responsibility, I found myself fully exposed to the people issues that often beset church life.

I'd like to be able to say that, having had the privilege of experiencing what I did, I have maintained a strong belief to this day, but that would not be true. In the first place, I could not maintain the exacting personal standards and thinking that is required to practice and to lead a Christian existence without me being seen as a hypocrite. Come all sinners and repent, but when you have, don't step out of line or the wrath of the church will descend upon you. Once in the club, you have to play by the rules. In any case, I was unprepared to deal with the serious strengths of feelings that people have that are difficult to deal with and are so divisive to churches – neither did I expect to. Such things, ultimately, undermine the whole thing here on earth. Whilst my family and I loved the fellowship of the good people in the church, I eventually put it behind me. Today, I guess, I reside within the agnostic camp, yet will often appear to others as ambivalent depending on the audience and the subject matter. Clearly, much good can and does arise from having such beliefs and I will always be prepared to fight their corner when I find that the teachings of the bible have been misunderstood.

ARMY SCHOOL OF AMMUNITION
WHEN FORGETTING CAN BE HARDER THAN REMEMBERING

By mid-1988 I had become the Senior Ammunition Technician at the Army School of Ammunition. Her Majesty the Queen visited the unit and it was a very proud moment for me when I had the opportunity to speak with her at lunch.

Time and time again, I'd watch as VIP visitors discussed the varnished boards, which listed all of our award winners, but none of those boards reflected the cost.

Lunch with Her Majesty. It was a very proud moment when Jen and I met
the Queen during her visit to the Army School of Ammunition in 1988.

In July during an operational tour, John Howard, a warrant officer instructor at the school, was killed in Belfast. He had been called to investigate an explosion that had occurred the night before, which had resulted in the deaths of two innocent civilians who had been passing by at the time. John was killed by a second device, primarily designed for him. He would be the last operator not to return from the long walk in that conflict.

Military staff of the Army School of Ammunition Kineton 1987. Lt Col Sean De Wolfe, the CO at the time, is centre of the front row. I'm to his left as the School's Senior Ammunition Technician. Major Terry Cosgrove to his right. John Howard is to my right at the end of the third row.

I knew John pretty well. I can tell you that he was an easy-going, pleasant guy: unassuming, well liked by everyone who knew him. He was neither particularly tough nor geeky. There was no 'side' to him and I know that he approached the tour with some trepidation that this type of work wasn't his forte. In many ways, he was probably the complete opposite of what Hollywood thinks a bomb disposal operator should act or be like. For me, John, epitomises all those guys who faced up to IEDs in the Northern Ireland campaign and didn't come back – ordinary men doing what most accept was an extraordinary job.

Perhaps John's death was the final straw; I can't remember now, but I do know that it was around that time that I made a decision. I wrote to the Senior Ammunition Technicians across the globe asking if they would support the need for a memorial to our dead. I consolidated the 100% positive responses into a letter, which I staffed to the then Commanding Officer of the Army School of Ammunition, Lt Col Des Townsend. He was sympathetic. His second-in-command, Major Terry Cosgrove, took the idea to the school graphics artist, Ray Gilder, who designed a memorial garden incorporating a statue of an operator. The corps and the Ammunition Technician profession ran with the idea and, through the efforts of many who raised the funds and because of those who kindly provided them, the EOD Memorial at Kineton in Warwickshire, true to Ray's drawing, was finally dedicated on 21st June 1991 at a service conducted by the chaplain general.

My friend and fellow 67B apprentice, Barry Johnson, read the first lesson at the service. Barry had been injured in an explosion attempting to defuse a PIRA

mortar and, for putting the safety of others before himself, he was awarded the George Cross.

A testament to ordinary but gallant men who entered a real dragon's den and gave their all for their country.

Displayed on the memorial is a name plaque for each operator killed since 1945. Behind each one of those plaques is another story that one day might get told. It's a story of ordinary people who, in the early days, with a minimum amount of training, entered a real dragon's den, left behind their family and friends and laid down their lives for their country. This memorial is for all time and for all to see – a tangible means by which this sacrifice can be recognised, respected and remembered.

It is sad for me to say, but on the day of the memorial's dedication only those who had been awarded medals were invited to appear in the group photograph. Insensitive? I think so, given that the families and other veterans were present. The controversy between those who were fortunate enough to be honoured by the system and our dead was not understood even then and perhaps, for many, it still isn't.

Going forward, will history record the glory of those honoured, or honour sufficiently our glorious dead?

The Northern Ireland campaign is over now. As I write, our people are carrying out this same work in other campaigns across the world and have been for some years. The equipment will be better, but the bombs are more numerous and the conflicts are much more intense. Even so, it will always be the Northern Ireland campaign that defined the IEDD profession, brought it to maturity and made it fit to fight the 'asymmetrical' type of wars of the twenty-first century.

Whether it was the boggy fields of South Armagh and County Fermanagh, or the urban environments of Belfast and Londonderry, the profession took on and dealt with everything PIRA could throw at it. In this way, the democratic line held firm whilst the politicians on both sides got their act together. For soldiers, this is always the nature of conflict. Holding that line, seventeen gallant operators serving with 321 EOD Company died doing, what is considered today, a heroic job, whose deaths went unrecognised by the honours and awards system. It was an aberration because everyone on our side, at the very least, has a lot to thank them for.

THE STAR SHIP ASTRID —1989–92

In 1989, I'm granted a Queen's Commission. I'm to become a late entry officer and begin life again as a lieutenant – from the top of a pile; back to the bottom, as it were.

The posting comes through and I'm provisionally earmarked for another tour in Germany. Not wanting to uproot my expanding family, the posting does not suit my plans. There is normally some flexibility on these matters and I mention my preference for a UK posting to Lt Col Townsend, who is still the CO. Not noted for hanging around, he immediately picks up the phone and, on my behalf, calls PB 9: the MoD department responsible for officer postings. As I peruse the artefacts dotted around the CO's office, the conversation with PB 9 seems to be going well when, all of a sudden, I hear the word 'ASTRID' mentioned. I stiffen. My heart misses a beat. I'm sure a cold sweat broke out on my brow. I lean towards him now, frantically waving my hands in a Wallace-type gesture, vigorously shaking my head and mouthing at the same time. 'No! No! No!' It is all to no avail, however, and, smiling back at me, the CO's telephone conversation continues apace.

Finally, he puts the phone down – the deed is done. He looks up at my traumatised expression. I swear he's laughing.

'Directorate of Logistics Information Systems at Bicester. Perfect – not far from where you live, isn't it?'

Already resigned to the answer, I ask, 'Not the ASTRID Project, surely to God?'

'Actually, yes. Ah, you'll be alright,' he says.

He means it. After all, it has been his generous, perhaps over-egged reports on my abilities that helped get me the commission in the first place. It seems he actually believes what he has written!

Why my trepidation? Well, the ASTRID Project (or the Star Ship ASTRID, as it was sometimes referred) was an MoD ammunition-related IT project that, at this time, had been stumbling along, through space as it were, for fifteen years. It had a reputation all of its own and was pretty much a graveyard for anyone posted onto it.

The first generation IT system, which had been delivered back in 1974 to manage and control ammunition, was pretty much flawed even then. The ASTRID system was to be the all-singing replacement. In point of fact, it had been a series of failed projects, each trying to deliver the same thing in a slightly different way.

If there is one lesson here, it is this: if your project fails or gets into serious difficulties, always change its name, otherwise your initiative will forever be associated with failure!

I had still to discover most of these things, so what is most agitating me now is that I would be required to qualify as a programmer analyst! Me? Oh my God! Here we go again!

Anyway, I scrape through the various IT-related courses and a commissioning course and finally arrive at Bicester to take up my post. It did occur to me then, and I'm sure I mentioned it to someone, that if you were serious about delivering a project of this nature you probably wouldn't have someone like me assigned to it – effectively an IT rookie! Anyway, as a mere lieutenant now I just got on with it.

Along the way, I get a trip to Germany to roll out some of the ASTRID hardware and take the opportunity to enter East Germany. After forty-five years, the checkpoints stand empty. The place is a real eye opener. Where any rebuilding had actually taken place since the Second World War, it was generally comprised of concrete and square in shape – no effort at aesthetics. The few shops we saw were extremely depressing and devoid of products. As for the utilities and pipes that in the UK are normally buried under the road, well, here they were on the surface alongside the roads, which were in a helluva unrepaired state – especially the autobahns of pock-marked concrete. The workers lived among the horrendously polluted byways and waterways at the industrial city of Helle – all the signs of a failed system. West Germany did indeed inherit a scrap yard when the wall finally came down.

On a couple of occasions, we are caught up in Russian convoys and getting this close to the 'auld' enemy is somewhat disconcerting.

We took the opportunity to visit the concentration camp at Buchenwald. On a bitterly cold day with snow on the ground, it was in many ways an extremely raw experience. We bump into more Russian soldiers when a group of them, some with families, are being shown around at the same time as us. Funny, I had never before imagined that Russian soldiers had families!

1990 Buchenwald Concentration camp in East Germany, the year after the wall came down. Strange feeling, mixing it with Russian soldiers.

One particular day at Bicester is ingrained on my mind. I remember it vividly, even today, all these years on. It was exceptionally hot and wearingly humid without any breeze at all. The air was heavy and oppressive. I remember discussing it with a colleague.

Unbeknown to me, on the demolition ground at Kineton, twenty-five miles away, a Sergeant Ammo Tech with a young Corporal Ammo Tech and another soldier were disposing of high-explosive shells one at a time – normally a routine task.

At the end of the working day, however, there was no sign of the group. Everything was laid out, prepared for the next demolition at the safe area, but the soldiers had vanished. It appeared to those arriving early on the scene as something akin to the Marie Celeste.

A search party was called for and eventually all three were found dead in a narrow tunnel at the bottom of one of the demolition pits. The subsequent investigation revealed that each shell had been placed by the sergeant to create an ever deeper tunnel. The depth of the tunnel was such that it took three of them to manhandle the shell to the end of the tunnel. The still, humid conditions meant that the gas from the previous explosion had not dispersed by the time the group arrived to set the next charge and they had all died from carbon monoxide poisoning. As I said earlier, the hazards from explosives are not always entirely obvious.

I knew the Corporal Ammo Tech; I had trained him when I had been an instructor at the school. For his marriage, I had lent him a gold and silver Ammo Tech badge to sew onto his 'blues' uniform.

I felt the need to attend the lad's funeral in Oldham where my overwhelming feeling was not just of sadness, but of shame. I felt we, as a profession, had let the families of those young soldiers down. The sergeant should have known better than to play games with these things, but our safety mechanisms and training had simply not worked to prevent such a disaster from happening. It was an avoidable tragedy, as they always are.

The following year, Project ASTRID failed to deliver for the umpteenth time. The rage of the Director General of Ordnance Services at the time and also the Director of Land Service Ammunition was palpable. They were informed that the Go Live would not be met and that at least another six months or so would be needed.

It got worse. When consultants were brought in to review the project, the general and the brigadier were even less enamoured to be informed that a further two to three years of effort remained before ASTRID would see the light of day. Oh dear!

ASTRID, at that time, exhibited all the classic weaknesses of a major IT-related undertaking that you hear about in the media from time to time. If the ASTRID system was ever to come of age, much of the project dynamic would have to change. Someone needed to get serious about delivering it.

This time they did. For a start, only experienced people would actually be employed on it – a breakthrough! The project methodology, called PRINCE, would be properly applied and there would be the necessary oversight. Phoenix-like, the Star Ship ASTRID rose out of the ashes and took to the skies again just as I was unexpectedly about to leave Bicester.

At this time, the world was a changing place; the Soviet Empire collapsed in 1989 and the Cold War was effectively over; the two Germany's were reunited and peace broke out for five minutes. To realise the financial benefit of this victory our Government offered thousands of British Army officers redundancy. Everyone who had portable skills, it seemed, took the money and ran. Thereby, it was that the collapse of the Soviet Empire became, for me, a lucky turn of events.

In 1991, I had only recently been promoted to captain when I received a phone call from the MoD at PB 9. They made me an offer I could hardly refuse: accept a posting to Didcot as the IT staff officer there and they would promote me to major!

The incumbent, Major Dick Gill, had opted for redundancy and none of the few remaining ATOs with IT qualifications who had been approached to take the job would touch it with a barge pole. Turning problems into opportunities is what often makes careers. So what could I say!

1991 - Twenty one years after we passed out from the college a reunion dinner near Oxford for the 67B Ammo Techs still in touch. Two ex 67B Royal Engineers joined us - Ged Gallagher and Phil Saunders. Barry Johnson had been awarded the George Cross, George Ferguson, two Queen's Gallantry medals and Des Kerr also a QGM.

DIRECTORATE OF LAND SERVICE AMMUNITION — IT BRANCH 1992–95

I took up the post in 1992, aware of grumbling from other ATO officers who were senior to me but still captains. They had a point, since I had effectively been promoted above them. But, I'm afraid, it is how the cookies in life occasionally crumble.

Dick Gill, with his eyes now eagerly set on civilian life, was kind enough to stick around long enough for me to be properly inducted into the job and he bestowed upon me his well-thumbed copy of the book Plain Words, for which I am eternally grateful; it is so important for a staff officer to write in a succinct and clear manner. Brevity is all important and that book was a brilliant start! Thanks Dick.

A short time after this, the Royal Army Ordnance Corps was amalgamated with others (including the 'auld' enemy, the Royal Pioneer Corps) and became the Royal Logistics Corps – or the 'really large corps' as some describe it. The RAOC is, therefore, no more. It is consigned to military history.

The job at Didcot was, as advertised, stressful at times, since a lot was expected, but then it was a time of change and it, too, needed to change. Keeping up to date with the relevant events so that very senior officers were properly briefed could be tough going, and no prisoners would be taken if you got things wrong. The profession was also struggling with a whole new bureaucracy that seemed to prevent us getting hold of desktop computers, which had quickly become the way forward. It was easy to get upset with people when things didn't go well or when forces outside your control did not seem to recognise your priorities.

I also had Project ASTRID to consider (but from the outside now), having been given instructions by the chief of staff, and also my boss, Lt Col Mike Watkins, to monitor it closely. I did and it did not always make me friends, particularly when I suspected the project was beginning to exhibit the poor practices of the past. Nonetheless, a man has to do... etc, etc. All those experiences have stood me in good stead ever since.

In 1994, the ASTRID system finally went live. Primarily, this was due to good project management, properly qualified IT resources, a business side bought in to the effort needed and appropriate senior level oversight. I like to think I also did my little bit to help pull it off.

1994 Leading lights from the ASTRID project have earned a stiff drink as the Director, Brigadier Roy Lennox, finally declares the system live after 20 years in development. I'm looking seriously nerdy by now. It is clearly time for a life change!

That same year, at forty-three years old, I feel I have achieved everything the service could offer in terms of ammunition management. I was at a threshold. Not to go meant I would never go. If I was ever to do something different with my life it had to be now. I had attended courses on, and had gained experience of, projects. I decide to market myself as an IT project manager and, in 1995, I retired from the army. My boss, Lt Col Mike Watkins, provided me with a great reference, which eased the transition into Civvy Street.

I had known Mike since we served together as corporals. He was now my boss and, when I first arrived at Didcot as a brand new, quite inexperienced major, it was his mentoring that enabled me to settle in quickly. I caught up with him again some time after I'd left the army to thank him for the help, which had undoubtedly oiled my way into civilian life. I remember him being quite animated about a project he and others were involved in. As the 'Durand Group', they intended to try and neutralise some of the enormous explosive mines that still exist today under the First World War battlefields in Belgium and France.

In the Great War, the front line was frequently stagnated for years, so it became a useful tactic to dig a tunnel and explode a massive explosive charge under the enemy. The enormous craters that remain for tourists to photograph today are evidence of how powerful these charges were. Many mines were successfully detonated, but some weren't and some never got to be used. Any number remain in situ to this day.

So, the project Mike and his team were involved in was to try and identify and then locate such a tunnel. Some of the mines are plotted on a map and so it's possible to guesstimate the tunnel direction. Digging down with a JCB and breaking into a tunnel would confirm it. Walking, sometimes crawling, along the tunnel would eventually bring you to the man-made, hollowed-out cavern directly under the German lines, as was. In that cavern, neatly stacked in sacks, would be the tons and tons of high-explosives lying undisturbed since being placed there by Sappers eighty-plus years ago

The first job of the team would be to locate the detonator pack in the centre of the stack, which they could expect to be deteriorated. Once that had been extracted and made safe, the sacks of explosives could be removed back down the tunnel and disposed of.

In February 1998, Mike and the team disarmed one large mine in this way.

On 11th August a second tunnel was identified near Vimy Ridge. The JCB gouged out a pit which broke into the tunnel. Mike dropped down to check it out, when, without any warning, the side of the pit collapsed on him and he was killed. As I say, if your luck runs out as an Ammo Tech it is likely to be final. I felt his loss deeply and still think of him from time to time.

At the entrance to the Canadian cemetery today, there is a memorial to Mike Watkins. Those who have passed by and glanced at the plaque might wish to know that he was one of the most senior active ATOs at the time, well respected by all of us and a great loss to the profession – one more good bloke that didn't make it to retirement.

When we look at the 'clag' that remains long after war and conflicts have finished, perhaps it isn't surprising that an Ammo Tech has become the last British casualty of the Great War.

ADAPTING TO CIVILIAN LIFE

Prior to leaving the army, I attended a number of resettlement courses and gained a Diploma in Administrative Management and also a British Computer Society Certificate in IT, both of which helped to pad out the CV somewhat.

On the outside now, I needed to understand a different way of working. For example, most businesses are fairly 'flat' with very little hierarchy. Within the service, you are effectively mandated to be listened to by the rank you hold; outside the service, such matters are much more ambiguous. I quickly dropped any reference to my previous rank; there is no need of it and it is, in any case, an alien concept to most people these days. A secret to achieving a successful career 'outside', I soon learned, is to provide value that has a discernible and positive impact on the 'bottom line'. This is what all businesses need, since they must accomplish it to protect their futures. The army, however, does not have to make a profit.

It's not that one system is right and the other not, but they are wholly different working environments with different sets of objectives. Soldiers will adapt more easily to Civvy Street once this fundamental principle is recognised.

A couple of jobs allowed me to adapt to civilian ways of working and hone my project management skills. In 2001, I applied for the job I have today, Senior Programme Manager, overseeing the board's portfolio of business critical projects. This involves getting them properly initiated and onto the tracks and then steering them to a successful conclusion. I support busy managers in their project-related endeavours. I also train business managers in the structured project management techniques and skills that they need in order to deliver business change successfully. To do all this, it helps to have a fairly process-driven mentality, much in common with the structured management environments of the ammunition business; even if the risks are incomparable! The skills I learned as an Ammo Tech were ultimately portable, but for less than obvious reasons!

TODAY

My marriage didn't survive long after I left the army. Jen and I separated in 2001 and we were divorced a short time later. Effectively, it let all the steam out of what had become a pressure cooker existence. I do, however, feel that the children's best interests were served by me moving on. Both of us have new partners now and the new status quo remains a much more amicable state of affairs. Our five children are called Isen, Estë, Beren, Emyn and Elendë – one of each I often say! If the names sound familiar to Tolkien fans it is because they are mainly taken from Tolkien's greater work, The Silmarillion. Nothing in life has made me more proud or has been as satisfying as watching them grow up. In turn, my hope is that the offspring of our profession can be proud of us and that this is especially so of the children of the men who walked into a dragon's den once too often. Notwithstanding their grievous loss, they can be as proud of their fathers as the profession is of them.

2010 - Paul and Ros into the future. Tripping the light fantastic.

I very much enjoyed a varied and exciting twenty-eight-year career in the army. It was quite a ride; sometimes it was very hard work; much of it was dangerous and, looking back on some of those events, I guess, I'm lucky to have survived it when others didn't. Close shaves, mishaps and the odd misdemeanour make for excellent anecdotes and many members of the profession have these in bucket loads. We all are, are we not, the summary of our experiences – good and bad.

I wouldn't have missed any part of my career for anything. For a Blackpool lad who left school at fifteen with little academic ability, not much ambition or thought for the future, well, I guess, I did Ok – more by good luck than any exceptional decision making by me.

That first chink of light broke through at the apprentice college, which caused a paradigm shift in my attitude to learning. It is the Ammo Tech profession as a whole I thank for providing me with the skills I utilise today.

The threats to civilised society from the Improvised Explosive Device will now be with us forever. The tactics are embedded in every extremist organisation's kill book. Such organisations have shown themselves to be pitiless and without mercy. The covert nuclear IED option draws ever closer since attack by missile is much too obvious to ever be considered a reality these days. And woe betide any nation implicated by the USA in such an attack. It is hard not to think that the world is sleepwalking towards Armageddon, ignoring the elephant in the corner of the room, hamstrung as it is by a weak international consensus.

All this means that the Ammo Tech profession isn't going to go out of fashion any time soon. The current generation of Ammo Techs have shown their courage, resilience and skills even under battlefield conditions. I think we are going to need them in greater numbers going forward; for they are a thin line and the skills they have are not learned overnight.

Today, we all have a lot to thank them for.

It is unlikely to change tomorrow.